Thank you for your purchase!

I ask that you please not share, modify, or resell any part of this workbook. Please direct your colleagues to our Amazon or Teachers Pay Teachers storefront. Thank you in advance for respecting the time and effort I put into creating these workbooks.

Ms. Daniela

Your purchase supports my classrooms and my family.
If you are happy with your order, please leave us a review on our Amazon storefront.

Connect with us on instagram @montessoriworkbook. We love to hear feedback and ideas for new workbooks!

The Phonics Skills Workbook provides comprehensive activities to help your child become a confident and resilient reader. This workbook is ideal for children who have experience working with both CVC and CCVC words. Activities include a review of essential skills such as phonological awareness, phonemic awareness, encoding and decoding. The aim is to establish a solid foundation before progressing to more advanced language skills such as long vowels, digraphs, and diphthongs.

The first section covers a range of **phonological awareness** exercises, including identifying initial letter sounds, compound words, and syllables.

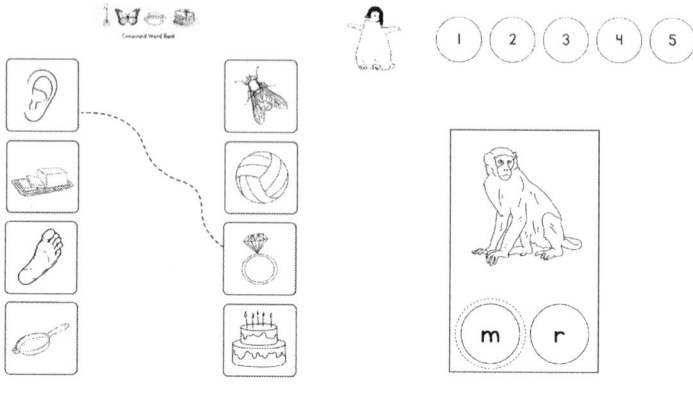

The following section focuses on **encoding**. It is designed to improve your child's phonemic awareness skills by practicing manipulating individual sounds within words.

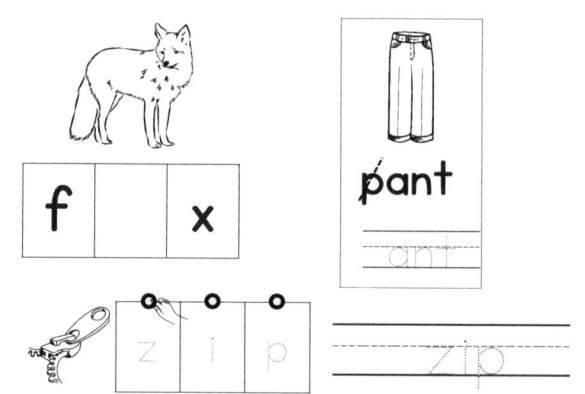

Once your child has mastered phonological and encoding skills, they can move on to the final section: **decoding**. This section focuses on the ability to turn written words into speech. You will find exercises to ensure your child is sounding out each sound in a word, rather than guessing based on context clues such as the beginning sound and surrounding images.

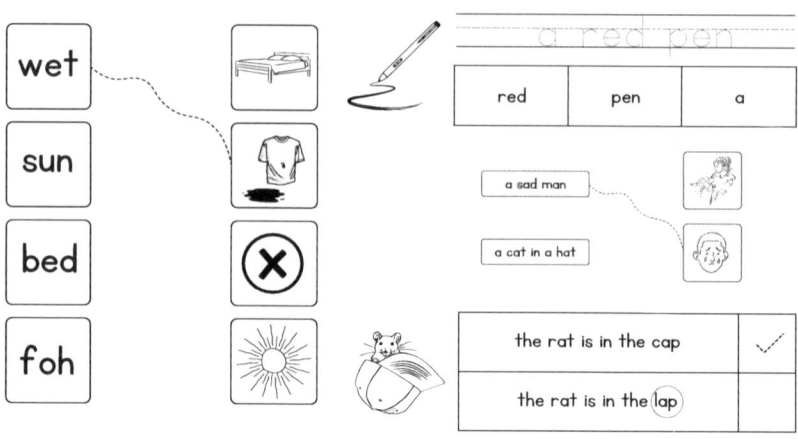

Fun at Home Activities!

Your child's reading ability is highly dependent on their ability to identify different sounds. Before or while engaging in the phonics exercises in this workbook, you can enhance your child's sound recognition skills by playing auditory games. One such game involves reading a sentence to your child and asking them to identify the number of individual words they hear. Your child can then mark the number of words they heard using a small object such as a coin, stone, or button. Start with sentences that contain two to five words and gradually increase the difficulty by adding words or using sentences with words that have two or three syllables. Once your child has mastered identifying words within a sentence, you can move on to identifying the number of phonemes or individual sounds in a word.

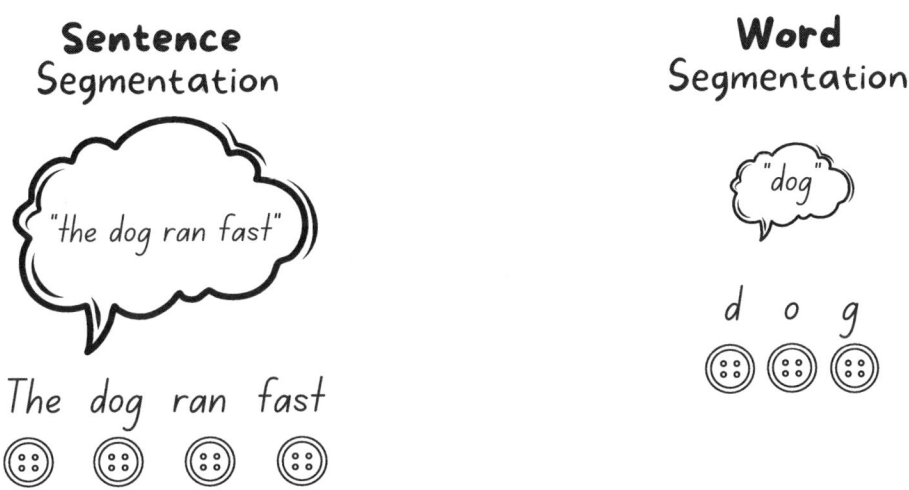

Sentence Segmentation

"the dog ran fast"

The dog ran fast

Word Segmentation

"dog"

d o g

You can make the games more engaging by swapping out objects. Some great examples include cheerios, themed erasers, sea shells, rocks, leaves, goldfish snacks, lego blocks, or marbles.

To make learning more engaging, try integrating large gross motor movements. Instead of using small objects, you can use mats (such as rugs, placemats, towels, or pillows) to create a game where your child hops between each mat to indicate the number of words in a sentence or the number of phonemes (sounds) in a word. This is a fun and interactive way to incorporate movement in learning!

"The dog ran fast"

d o g

Substituting
Phonemes

Another game you can play is replacing phonemes (sounds) in a word. You will change a letter sound and ask your child to guess the new sound.

adult: what are the three sounds in this word - cat?
child: /c/ /a/ /t/

adult: what happens if we change /c/ to /r/?
child: it says rat

Isolating
Phonemes

What is the first sound you hear in rug? What is the second sound you hear in pot? What is the last sound you hear in bun?

Deleting
Phonemes

bat - What word do we get when we take away /b/?

Adding
Phonemes

What word do you get when you add /p/ to /ig/ ?

Rhyming

Encourage your child to practice their rhyming skills by inventing rhyming words aloud. Start with a rhyming song or book as a warm-up exercise, then ask them to create rhyming words. The words can be silly or real. My students love coming up with silly rhyming words.

adult: what rhymes with ring?
child: sing, ping, ling, cring, ping, bling, gling...

I Spy

I Spy something in the room that starts with /p/... you are right it is the pillow!

I Spy an animal that makes the sound moo ... you are right it is the cow!

I Spy a toy that ends with /s/ ... you are right it is the bus!

| Table of Contents |

Email me at

ms.daniela@montessoriworkbook.com

for a cut and paste extension.

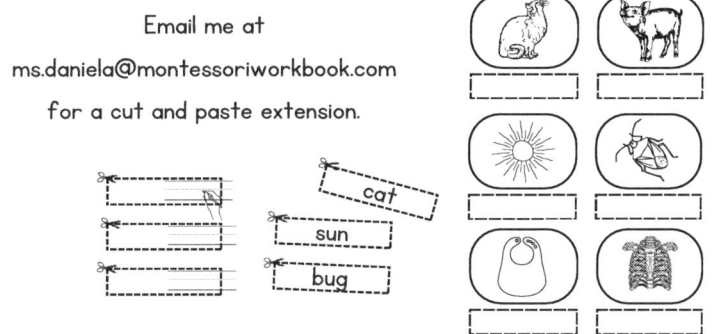

Say the word and clap out the syllables. Circle the correct number of syllables.

1   2   3   4   5

1   2   3   4   5

1   2   3   4   5

1   2   3   4   5

1   2   3   4   5

1

Say the word and clap out the syllables. Circle the correct number of syllables.

Say the word and clap out the syllables. Circle the correct number of syllables.

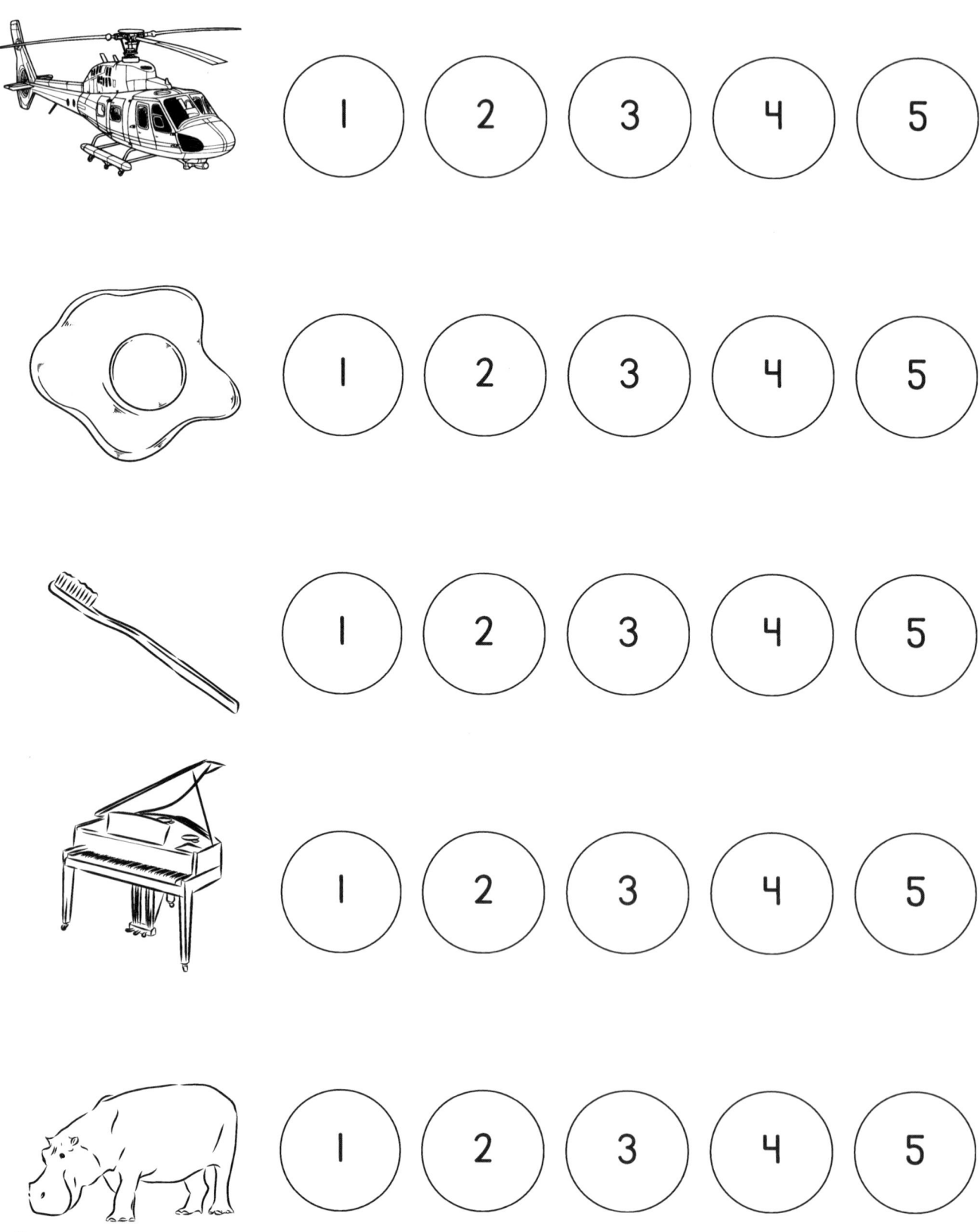

3

Say the word and clap out the syllables. Circle the correct number of syllables.

Draw a line to match the two words that create a compound word.

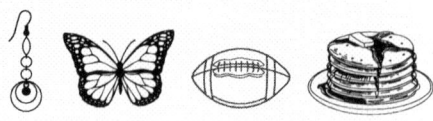

Compound Word Bank

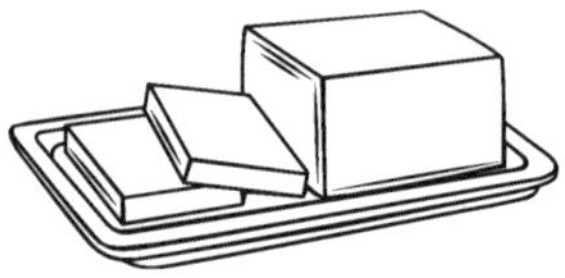

Draw a line to match the two words that create a compound word.

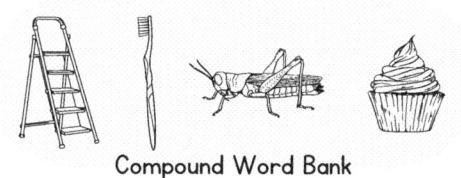
Compound Word Bank

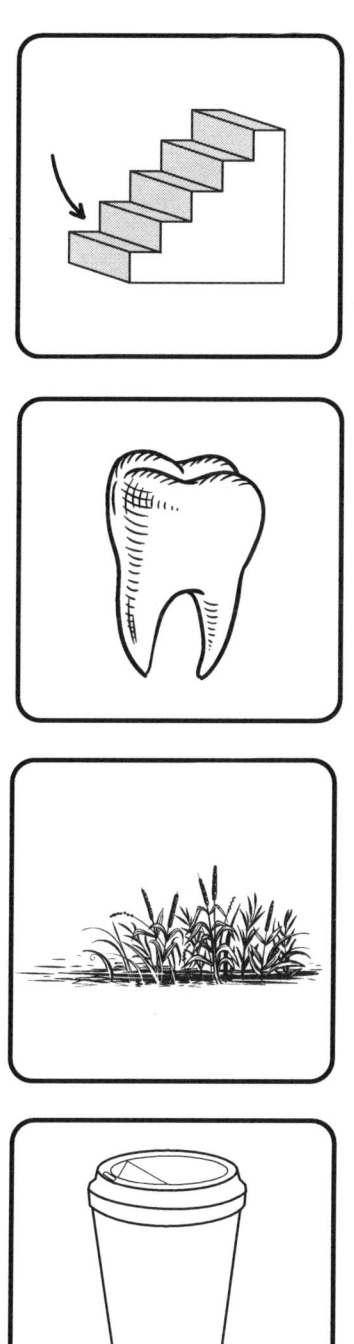

6

Draw a line to match the two words that create a compound word.

Compound Word Bank

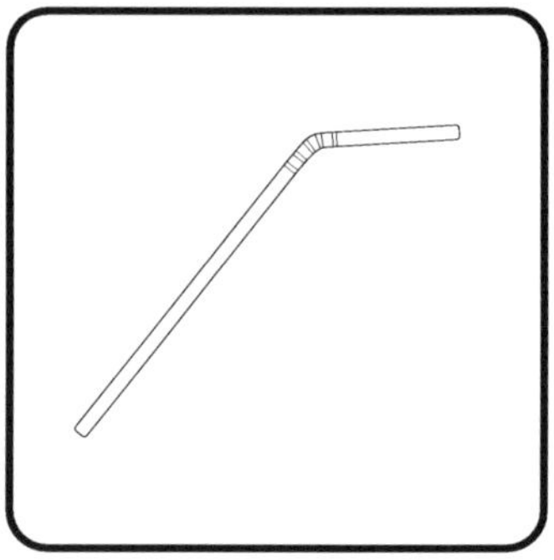

7

Draw a line to match the two words that create a compound word.

Compound Word Bank

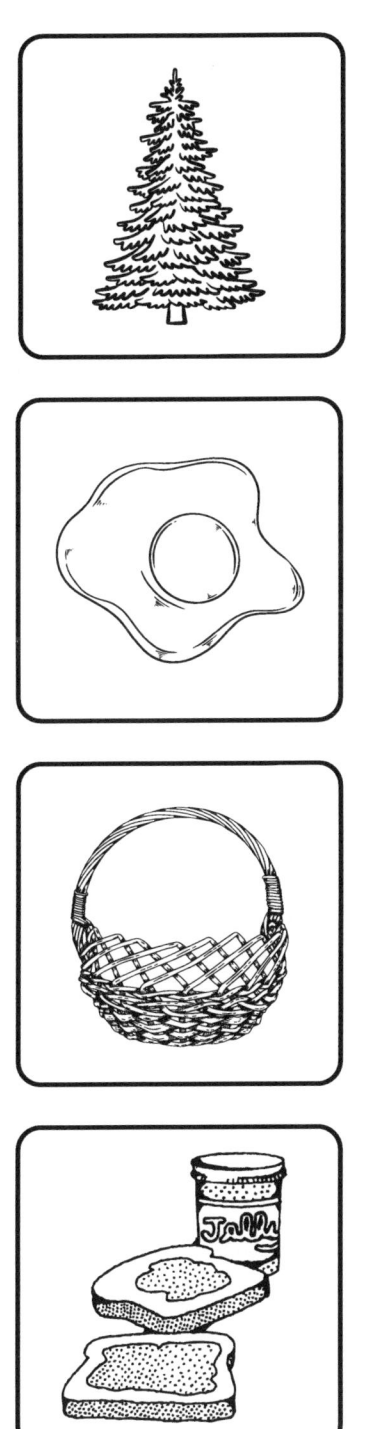

8

Draw a line to match the two words that create a compound word.

Compound Word Bank

9

Draw a line to match the two words that create a compound word.

Compound Word Bank

10

Draw a line to match the two words that create a compound word.

Compound Word Bank

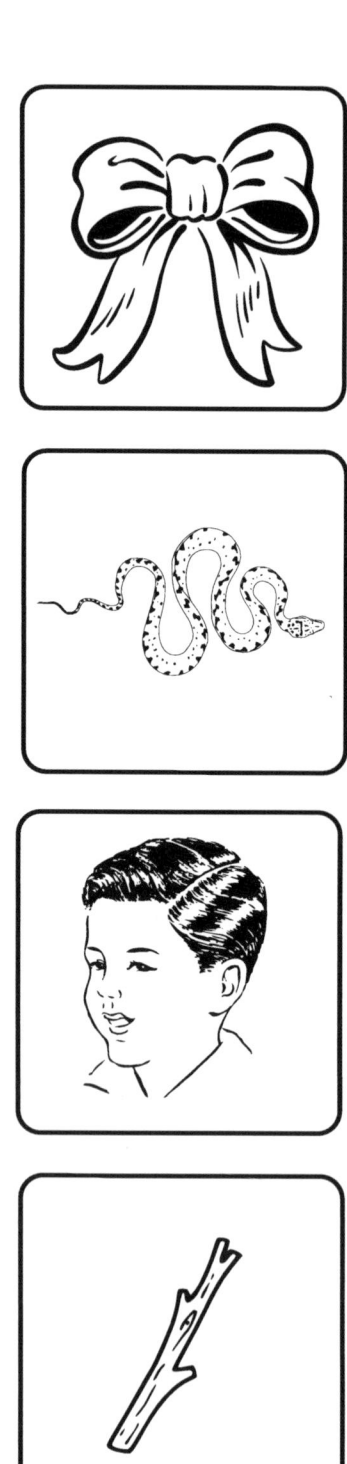

II

Draw a line to match the two words that create a compound word.

Compound Word Bank

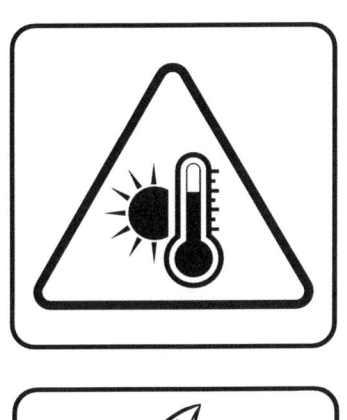

Draw a line to match the two words that create a compound word.

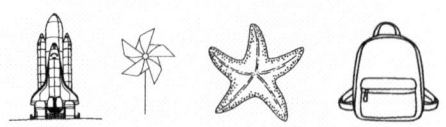

Compound Word Bank

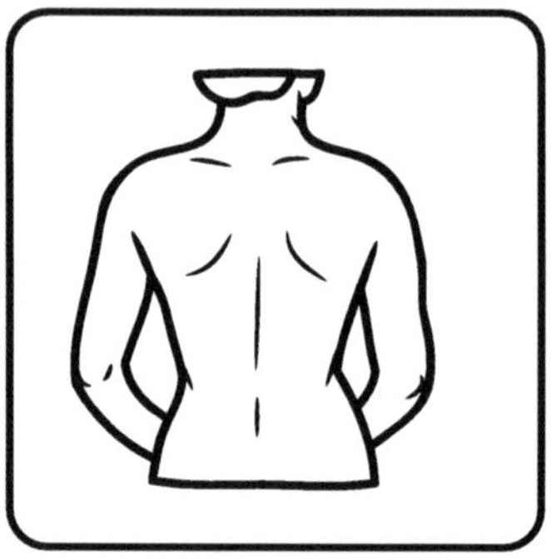

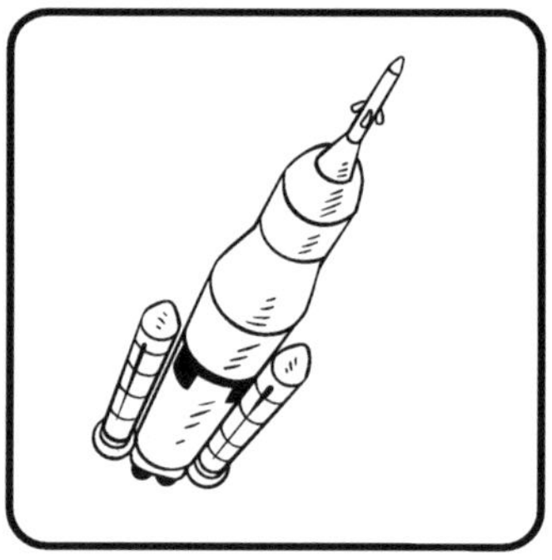

13

Circle the correct beginning sound.

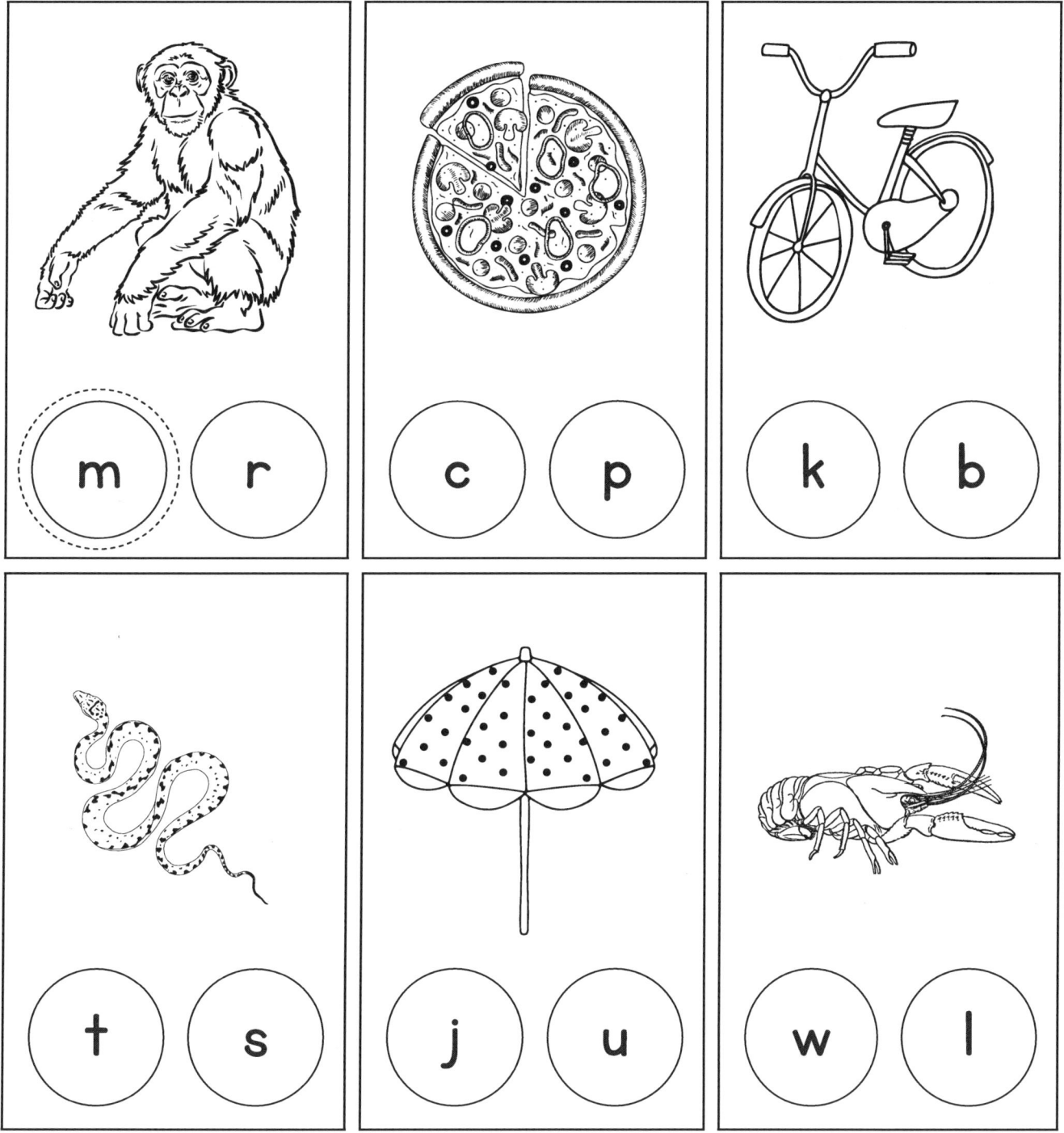

m   r

c   p

k   b

t   s

j   u

w   l

Circle the correct beginning sound.

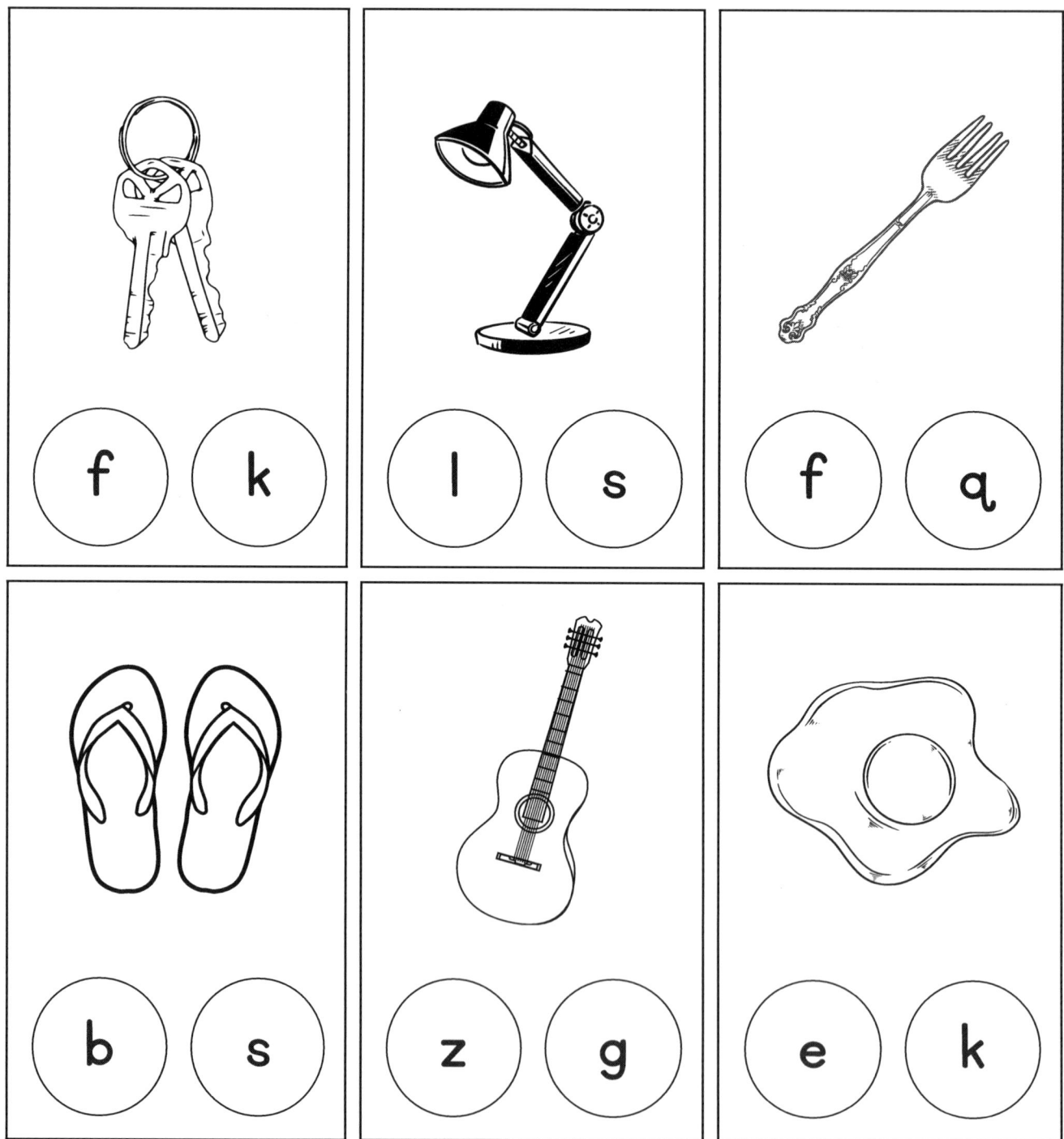

Circle the correct beginning sound.

16

Circle the correct beginning sound.

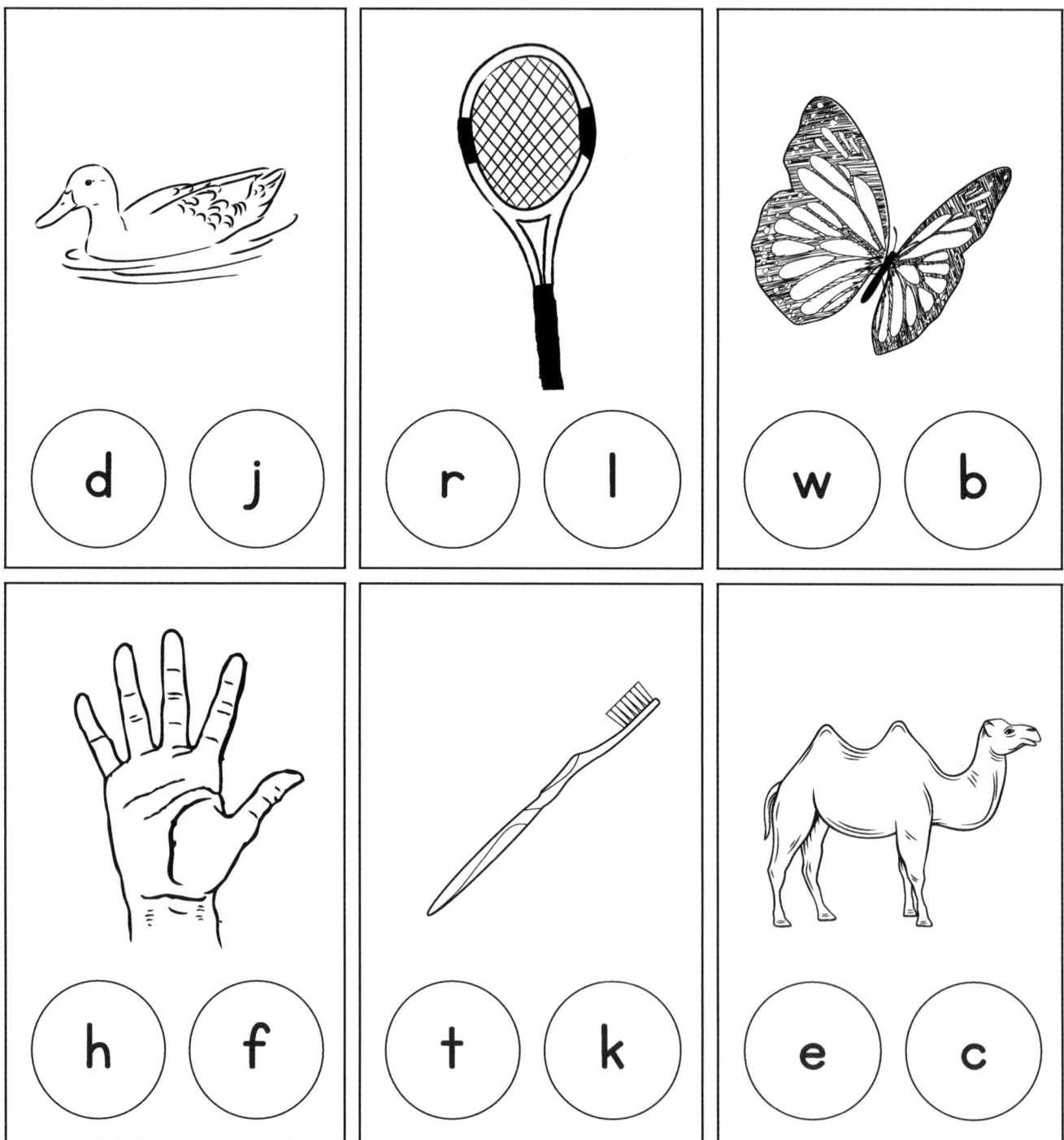

Circle the correct beginning sound.

Circle the correct beginning sound.

Circle the correct beginning sound.

m   t   h   p   a   e

u   z   i   n   j   w

Circle the correct beginning sound.

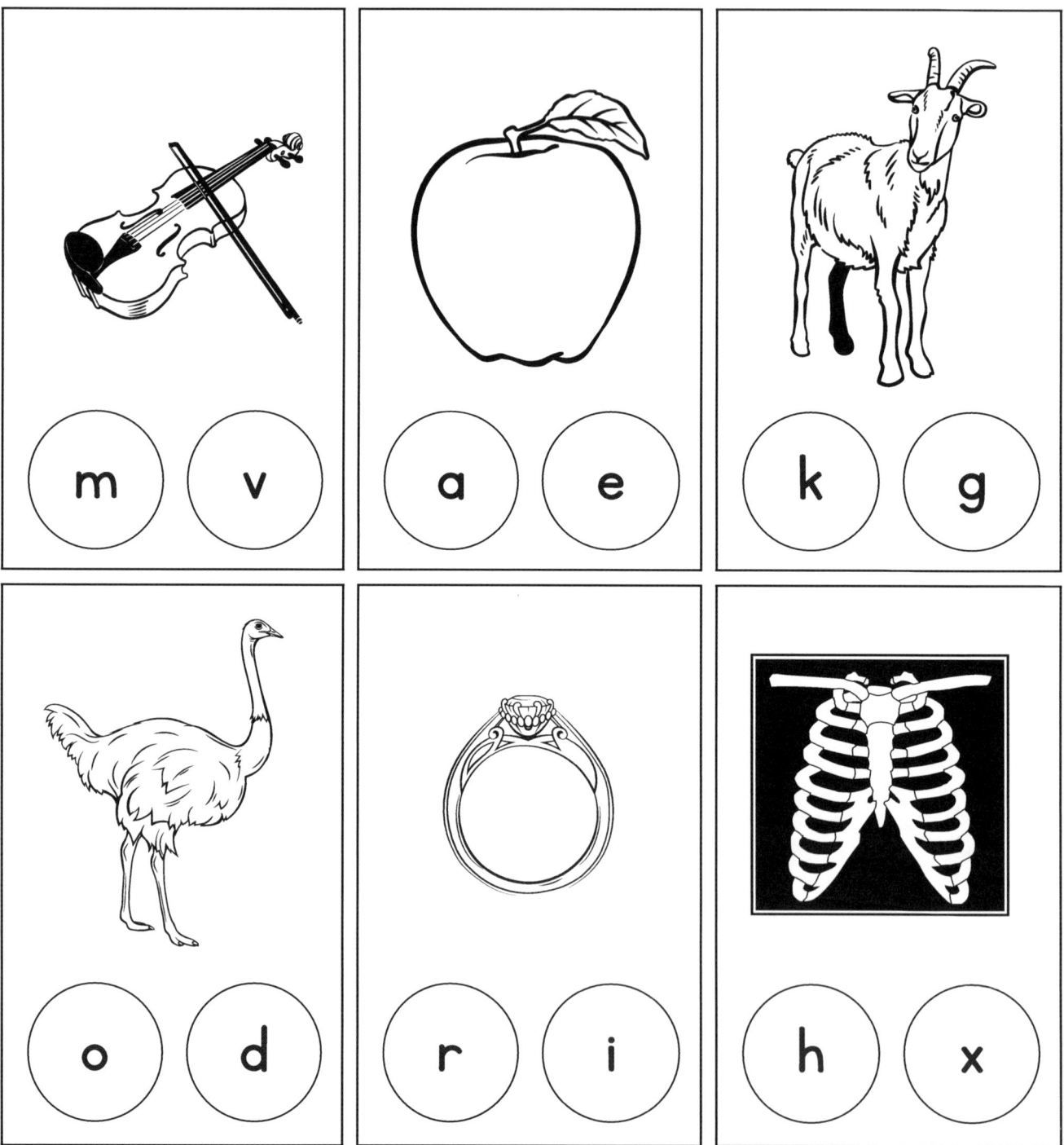

Circle the correct beginning sound.

z   v

t   v

j   c

t   d

y   r

p   w

22

Write the correct middle sound for each word.

a e i o u

p	i	g

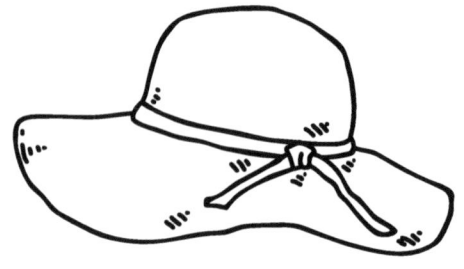

h		t

c		t

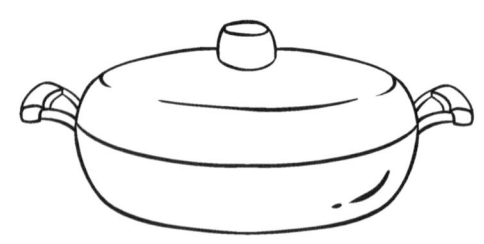

p		t

Write the correct middle sound for each word.

a e i o u

v		n

p		n

PARKING
ZONE

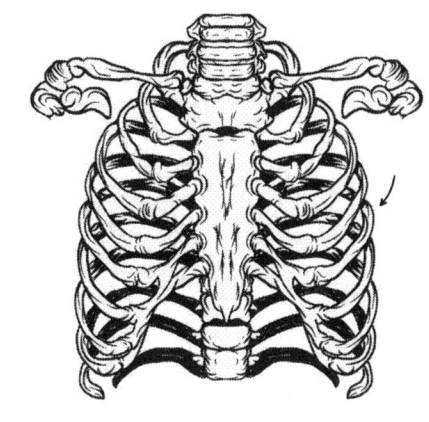

l		t

r		b

24

Write the correct middle sound for each word.

a	e	i	o	u

r		t

h		n

s		n

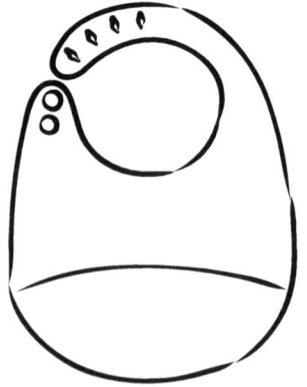

b		b

Write the correct middle sound for each word.

| a | e | i | o | u |

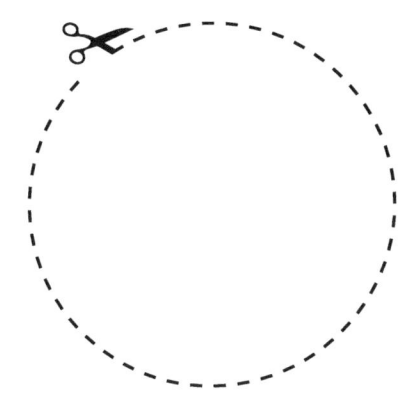

c		t

l		g

f		n

h		m

26

Write the correct middle sound for each word.

a e i o u

c		n

m		m

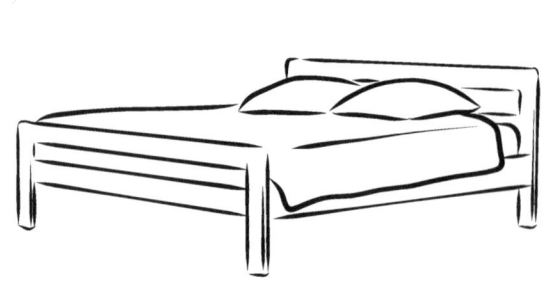

b		d

r		n

Write the correct middle sound for each word.

| a | e | i | o | u |

| w | | g |

| m | | t |

| c | | b |

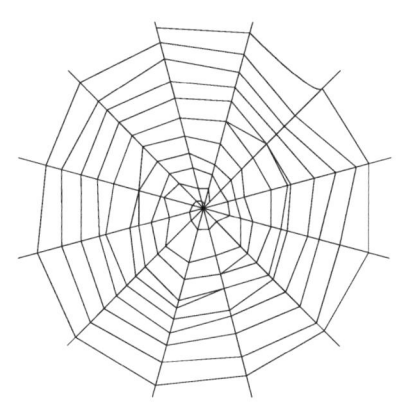

| w | | b |

28

Write the correct middle sound for each word.

| a | e | i | o | u |

c		g

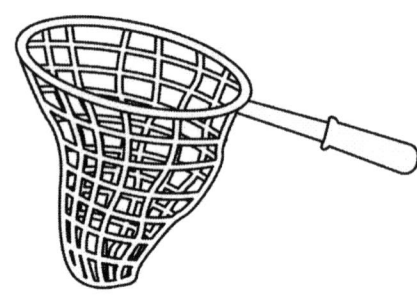

n		t

n		t

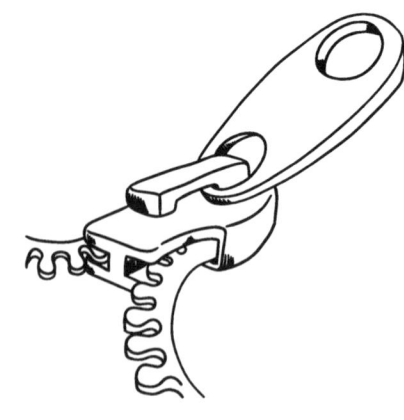

z		p

29

Write the correct middle sound for each word.

| a | e | i | o | u |

f		x

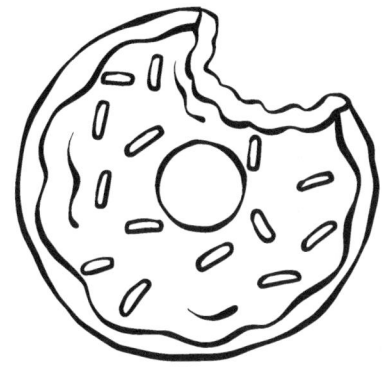

b		t

t		n

m		g

Write the correct middle sound for each word.

| a | e | i | o | u |

| b | | n |

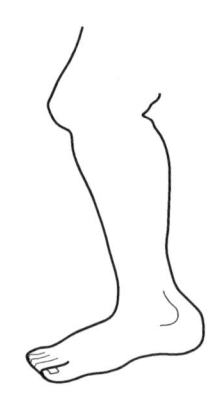

| l | | g |

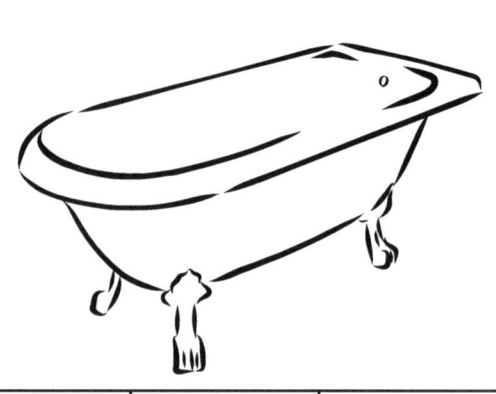

| t | | b |

| b | | g |

31

Write the correct middle sound for each word.

a e i o u

m		p

w		t

s		d

l		d

Write the correct middle sound for each word.

a e i o u

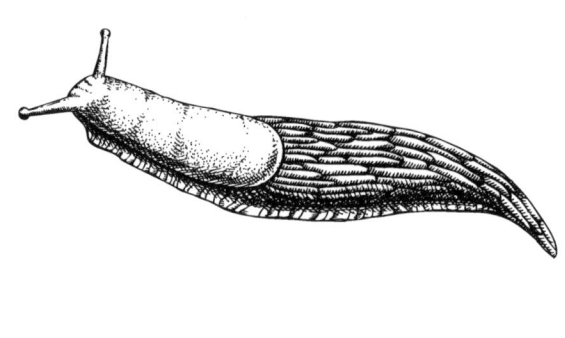

| s | l | | g |

| f | r | | g |

| t | w | | g |

| f | l | | t |

33

Write the correct middle sound for each word.

a e i o u

s	w		m

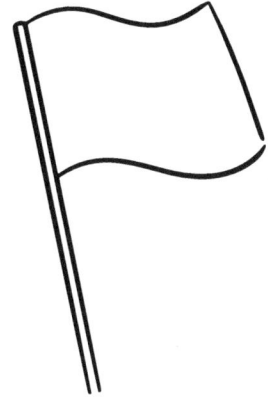

f	l		g

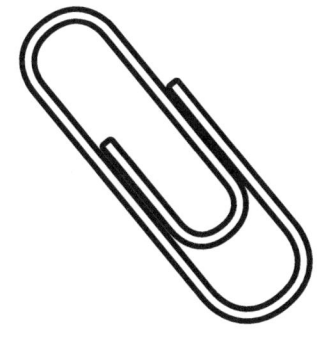

c	l		p

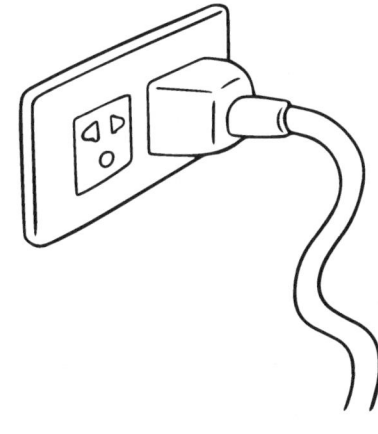

p	l		g

Write the correct middle sound for each word.

a e i o u

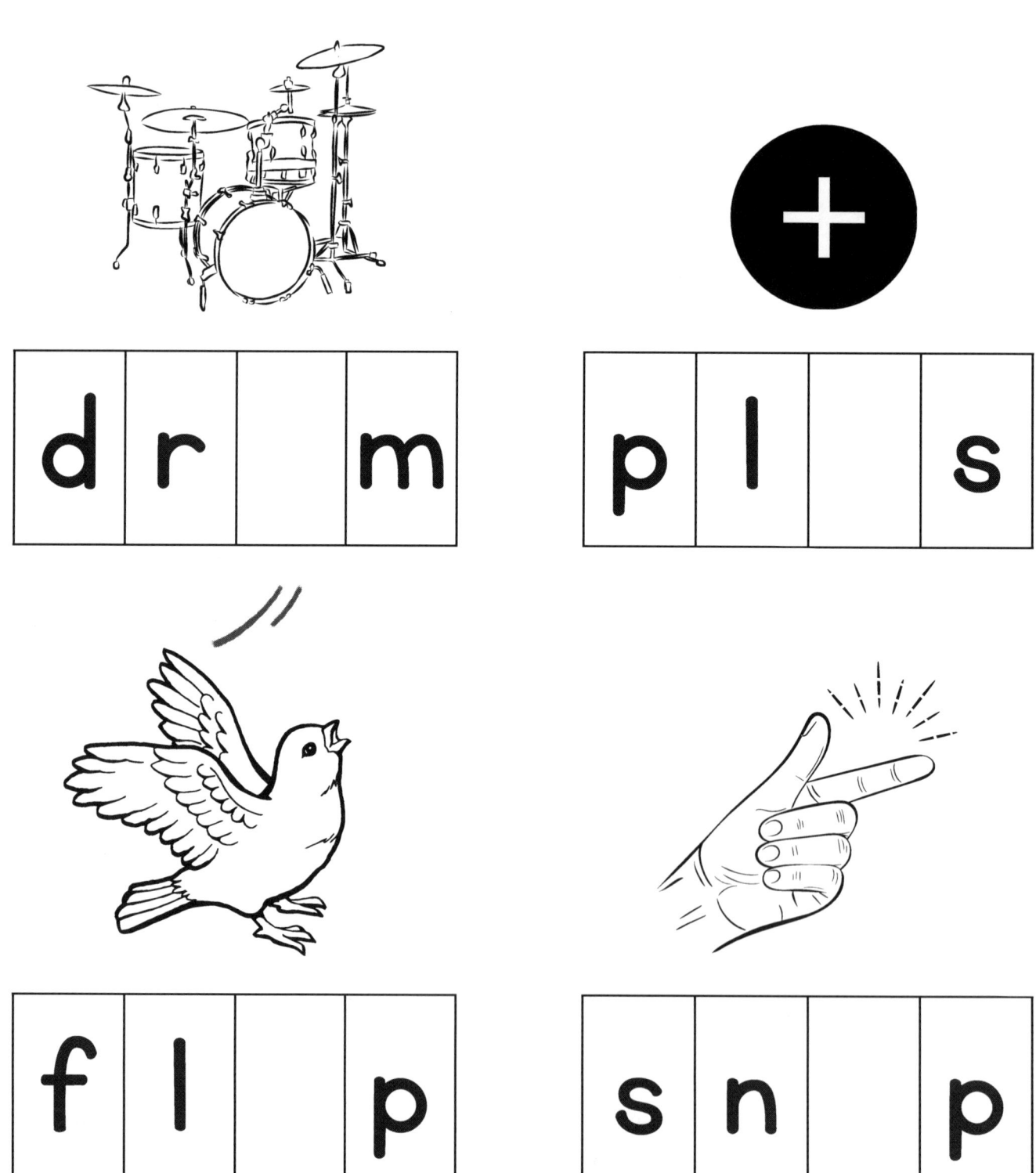

| d | r | | m |

| p | l | | s |

| f | l | | p |

| s | n | | p |

Write the correct middle sound for each word.

a e i o u

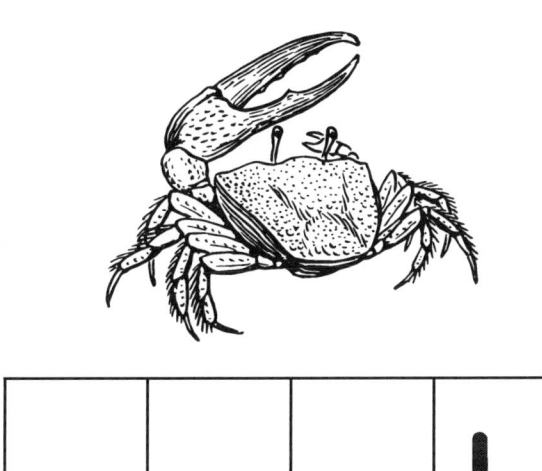

c	r		b

p	l		m

s	l		p

c	r		b

36

Write the correct ending sound for each word.

b c d f g h j k l m n p q r s t v w x y z

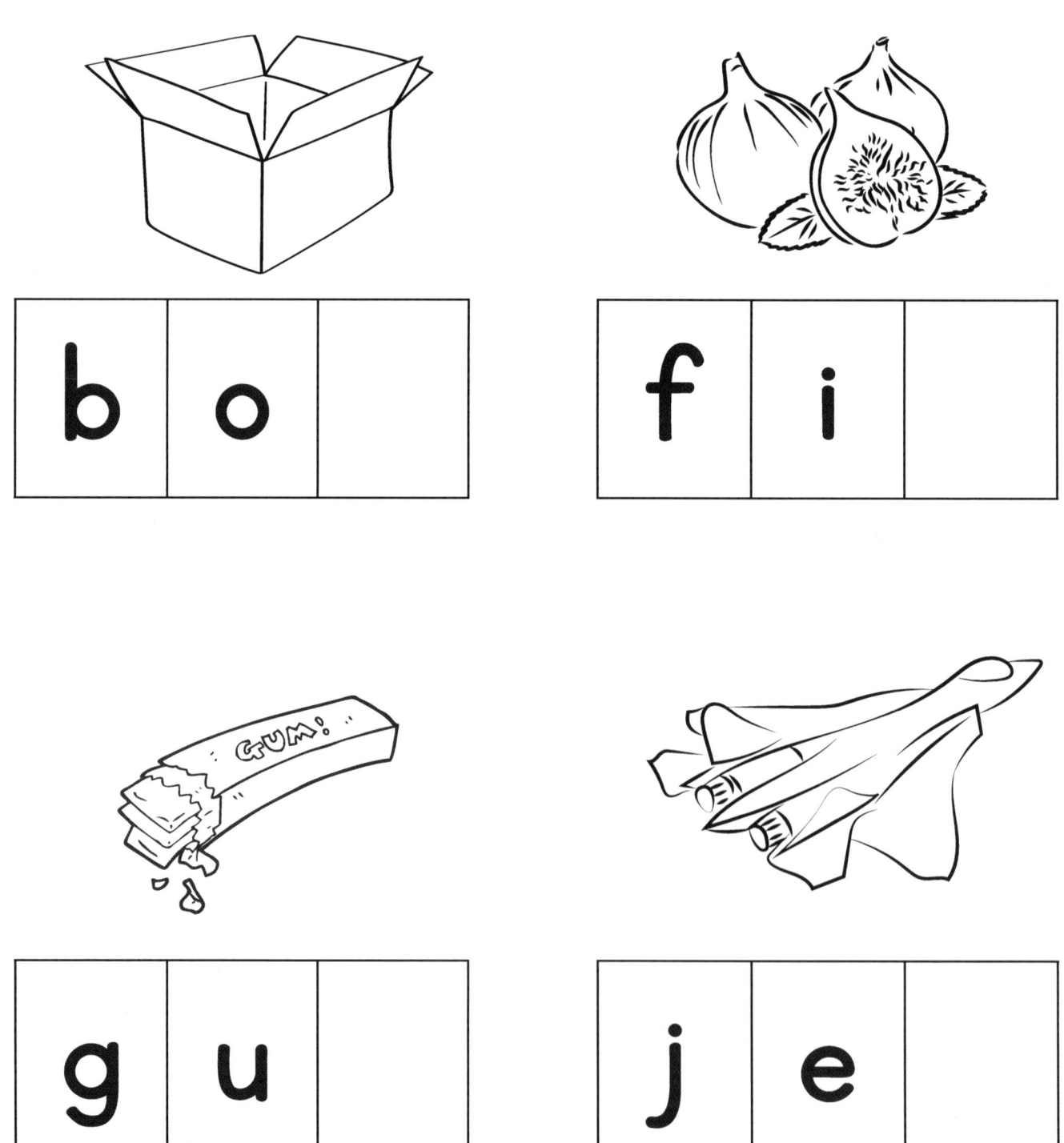

| b | o | |

| f | i | |

| g | u | |

| j | e | |

Write the correct ending sound for each word.

b c d f g h j k l m n p q r s t v w x y z

| d | a | |

| r | u | |

| n | a | |

| b | a | |

Write the correct ending sound for each word.

b c d f g h j k l m n p q r s t v w x y z

| b | u | |

| j | a | |

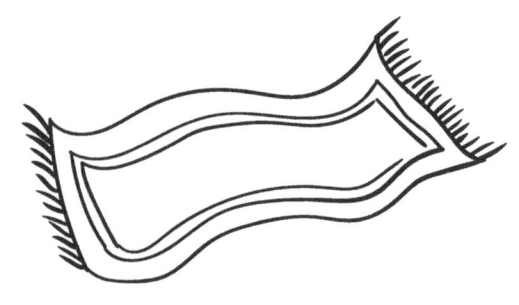

| r | u | |

| b | u | |

39

Write the correct ending sound for each word.

| b | c | d | f | g | h | j | k | l | m | n | p | q | r | s | t | v | w | x | y | z |

| h | u | |

| m | a | |

| w | a | |

| w | i | |

40

Write the correct ending sound for each word.

b c d f g h j k l m n p q r s t v w x y z

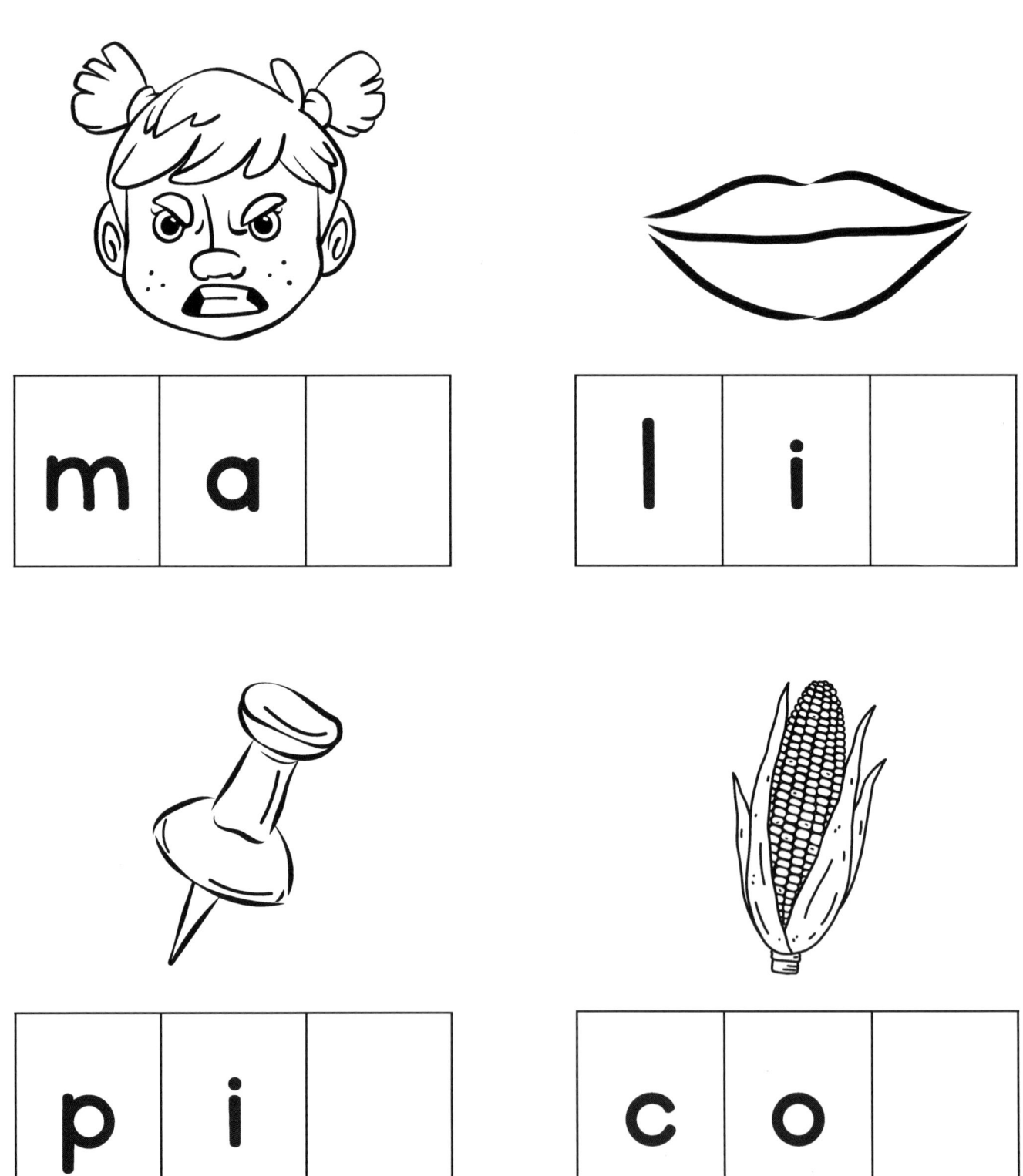

m a

l i

p i

c o

41

Write the correct ending sound for each word.

b c d f g h j k l m n p q r s t v w x y z

| t | o | |

| r | a | |

| k | i | |

| b | u | |

42

Write the correct ending sound for each word.

b c d f g h j k l m n p q r s t v w x y z

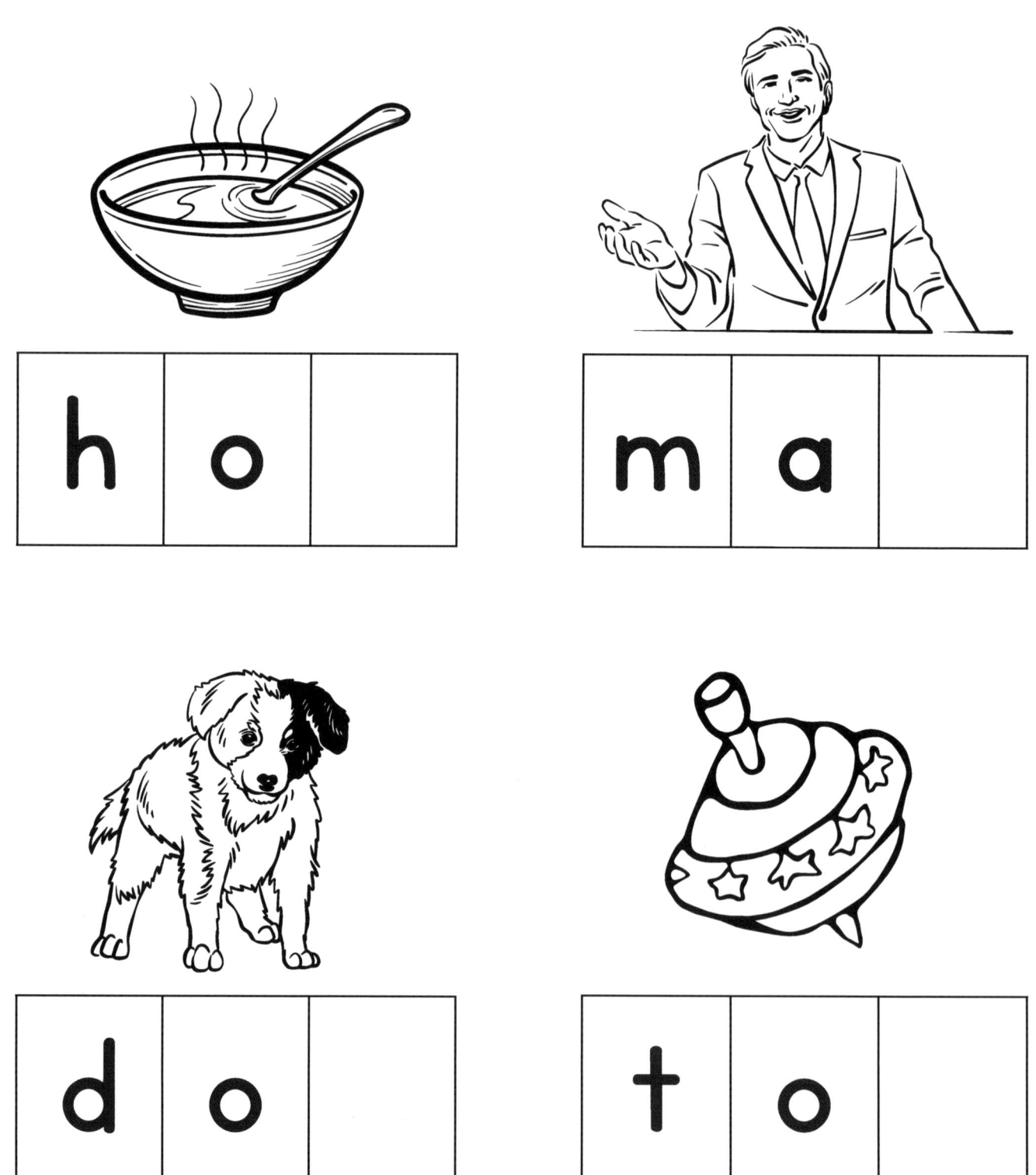

| h | o | |

| m | a | |

| d | o | |

| t | o | |

Write the correct ending sound for each word.

b c d f g h j k l m n p q r s t v w x y z

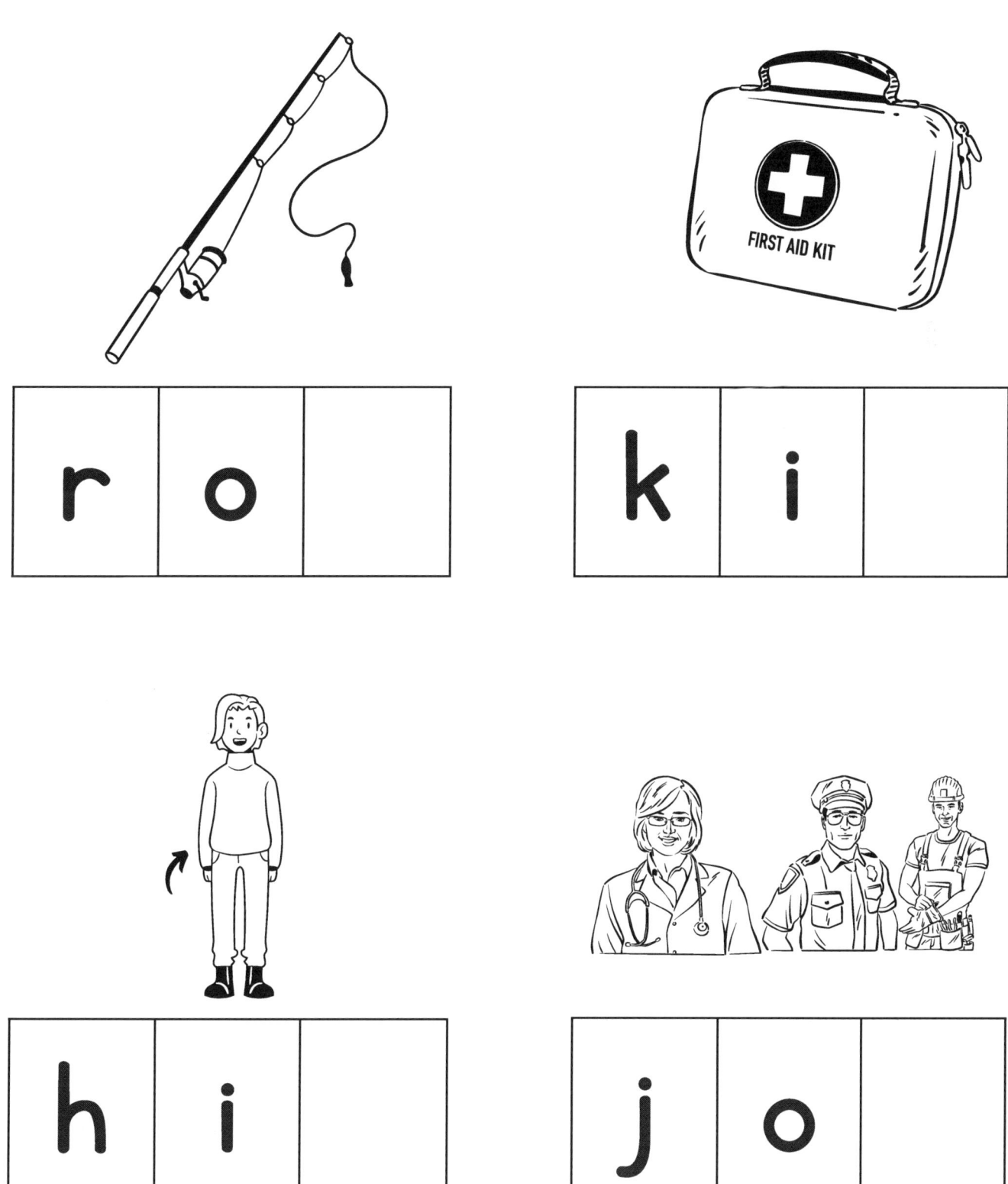

| r | o | |

| k | i | |

| h | i | |

| j | o | |

Write the correct ending sound for each word.

b c d f g h j k l m n p q r s t v w x y z

d o

h u

y a

p o

45

Write the correct ending sound for each word.

b c d f g h j k l m n p q r s t v w x y z

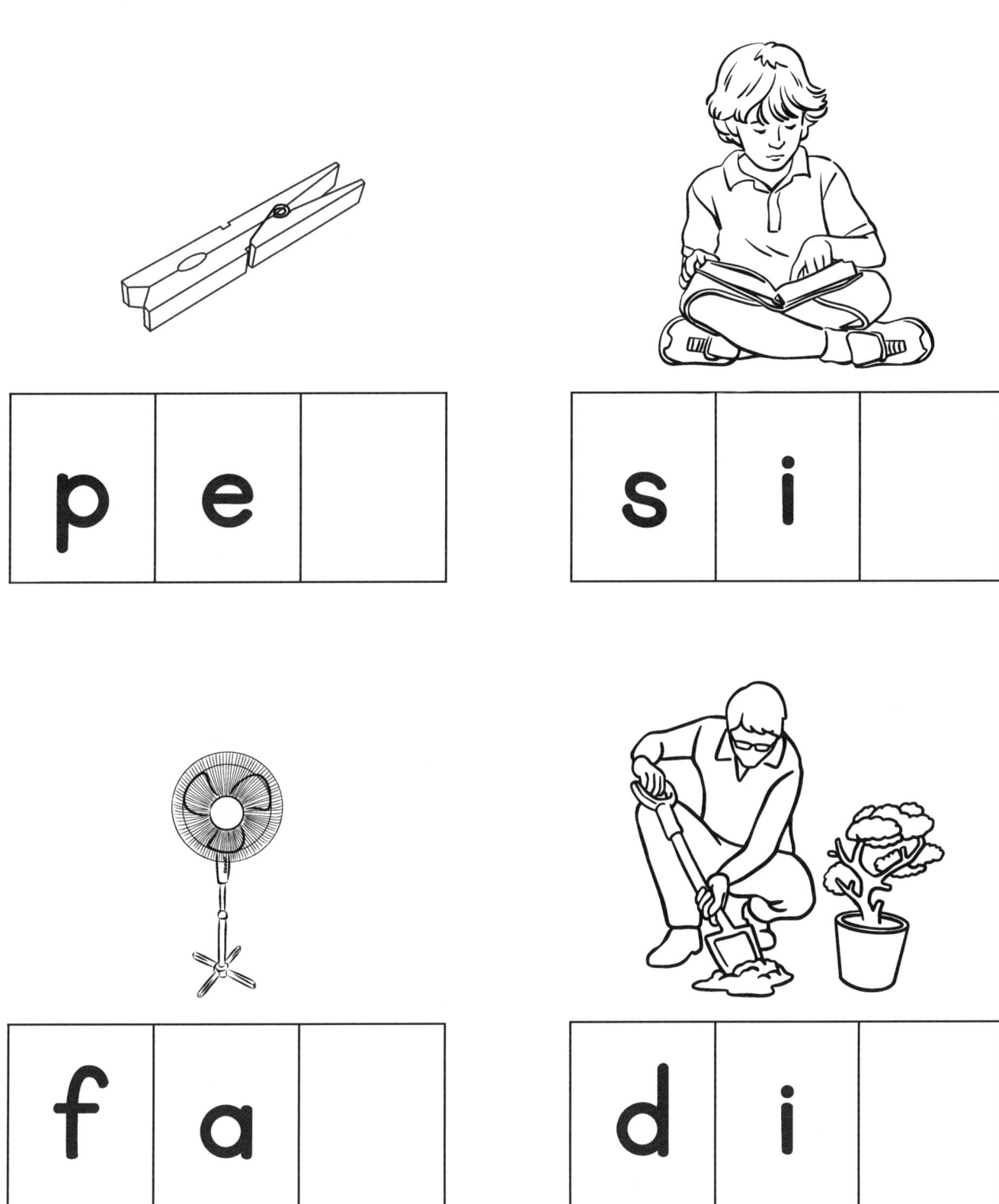

| p | e | |

| s | i | |

| f | a | |

| d | i | |

46

Write the correct ending sound for each word.

b c d f g h j k l m n p q r s t v w x y z

n e | |

j u | |

h a | |

s a | |

Write the correct ending sound for each word.

b c d f g h j k l m n p q r s t v w x y z

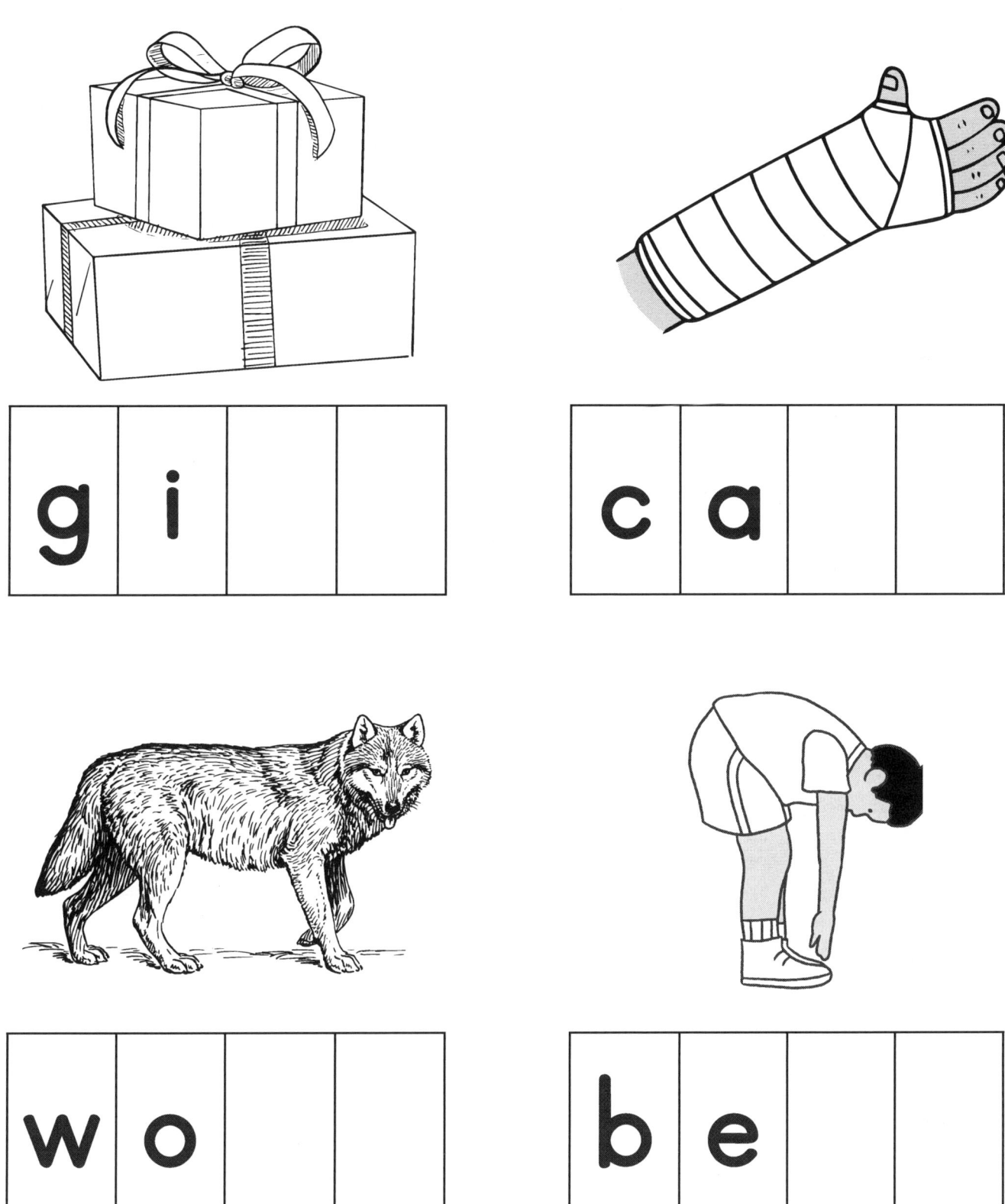

| g | i | | |

| c | a | | |

| w | o | | |

| b | e | | |

48

Write the correct ending sound for each word.

b c d f g h j k l m n p q r s t v w x y z

| m | e | | |

| t | e | | |

| r | a | | |

| g | o | | |

Write the <u>middle sound</u> for each word. Make a check mark if they are the same and X if they are different

a	✓	a	
e	✗	o	

Change the <u>beginning</u> sound of each word to create the new word.

log   d o g

bun

cat

mug

net

hip

Change the <u>beginning</u> sound of each word to create the new word.

man →

dig →

mop →

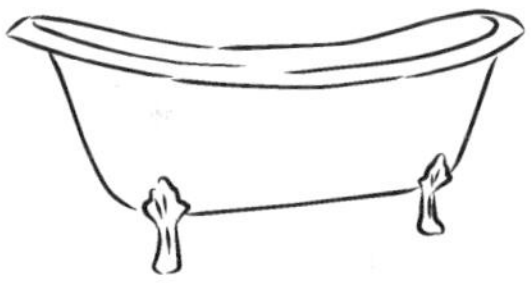

cub →

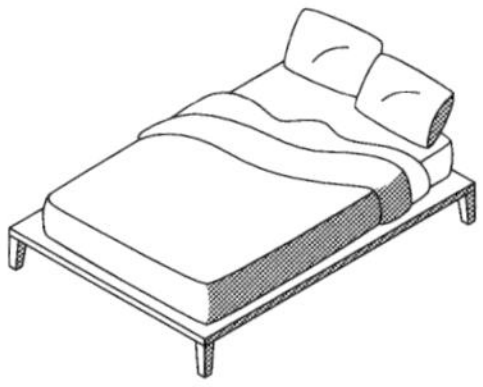

red →

wag →

Remove the <u>ending</u> sound of each word to create the new word.

start → star

plant → _____

clamp → _____

tent → _____

band → _____

card → _____

53

Remove the <u>beginning</u> sound of each word to create the new word.

pant _____	clip _____
stop _____	drip _____
clap _____	twig _____

Map it, Graph it & Write it

First, tap your finger on each circle for each sound in the word. Next, write each individual sound in the boxes. Finally, write the complete word in the lines provided.

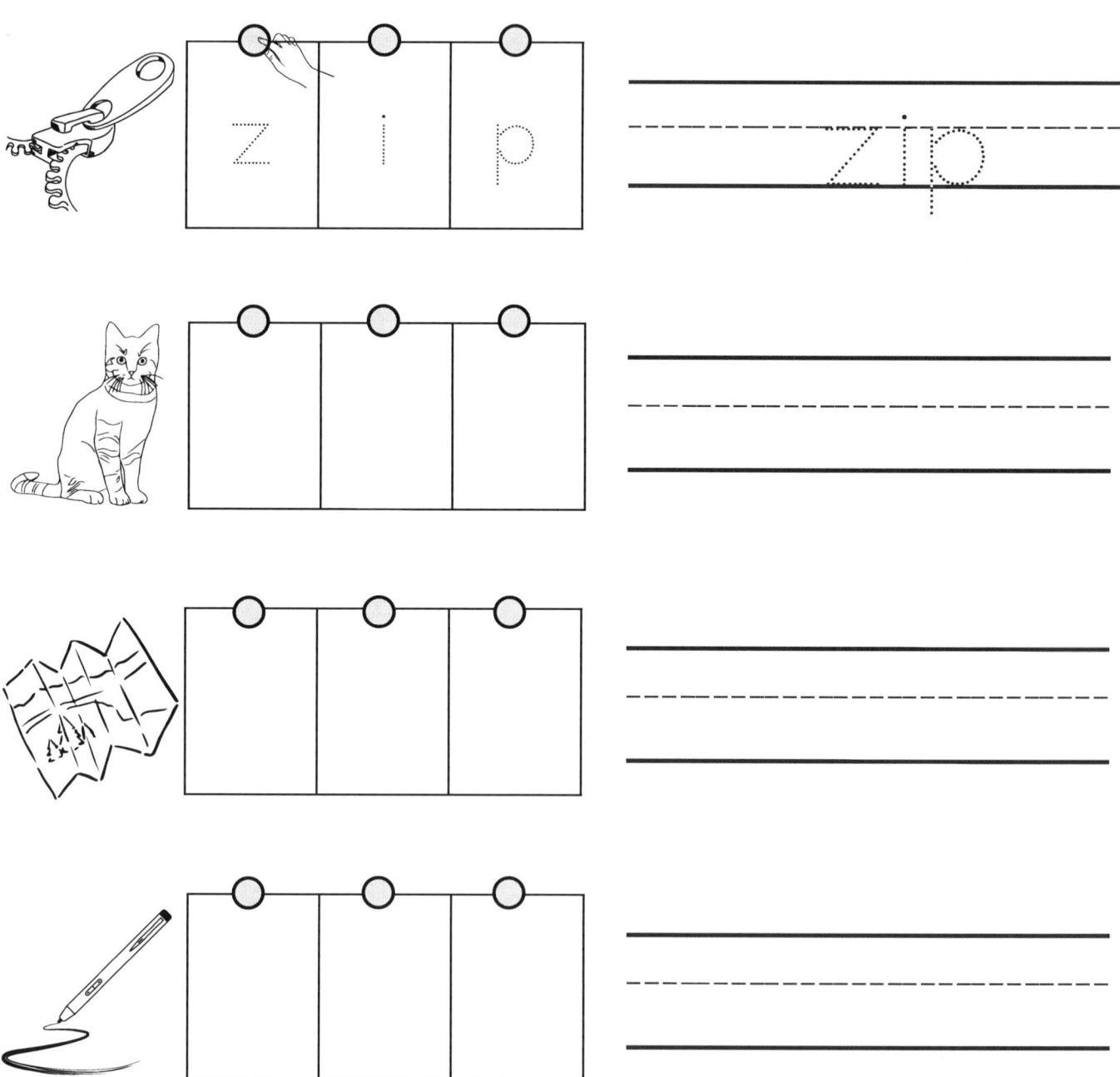

Map it, Graph it & Write it

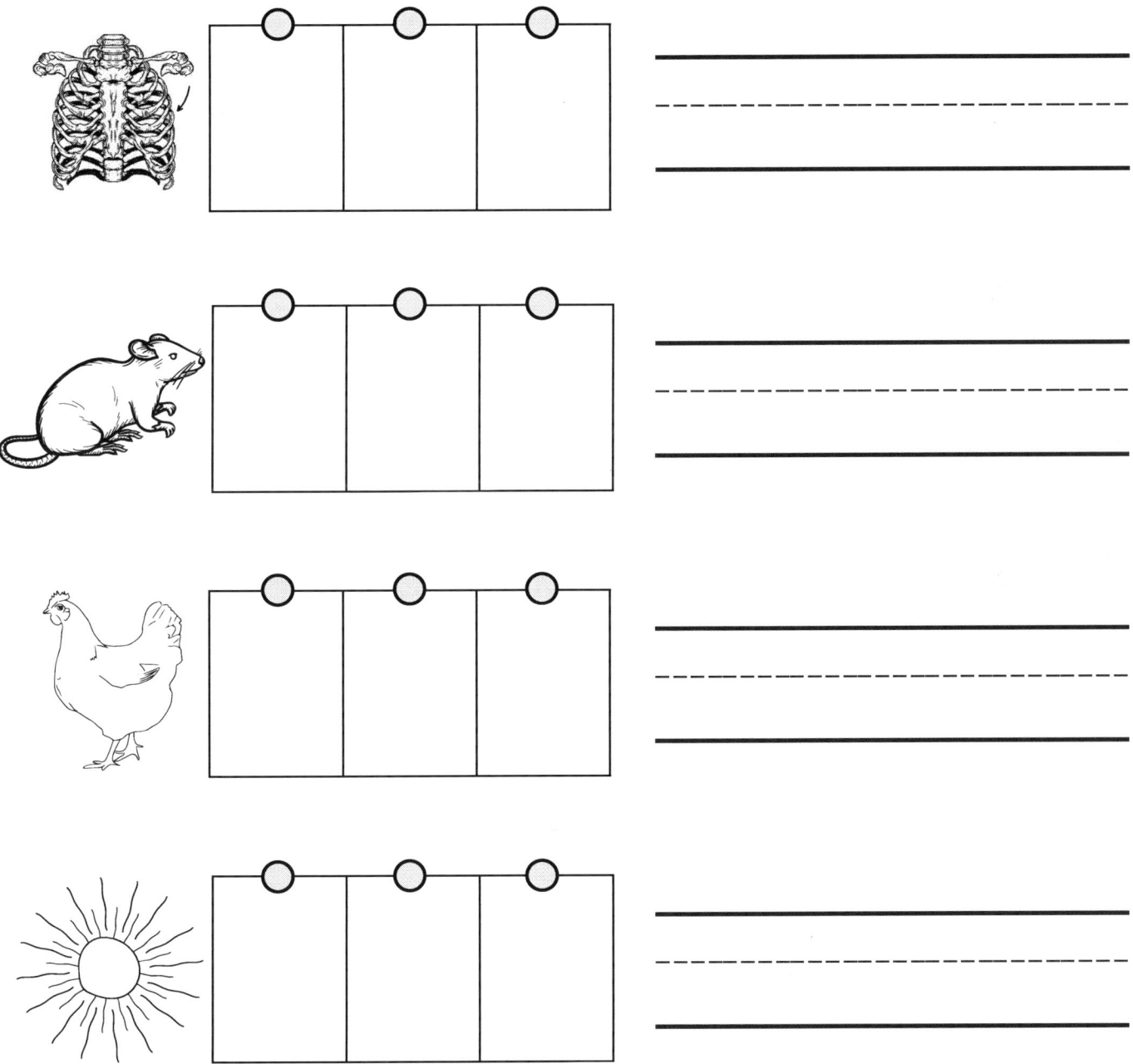

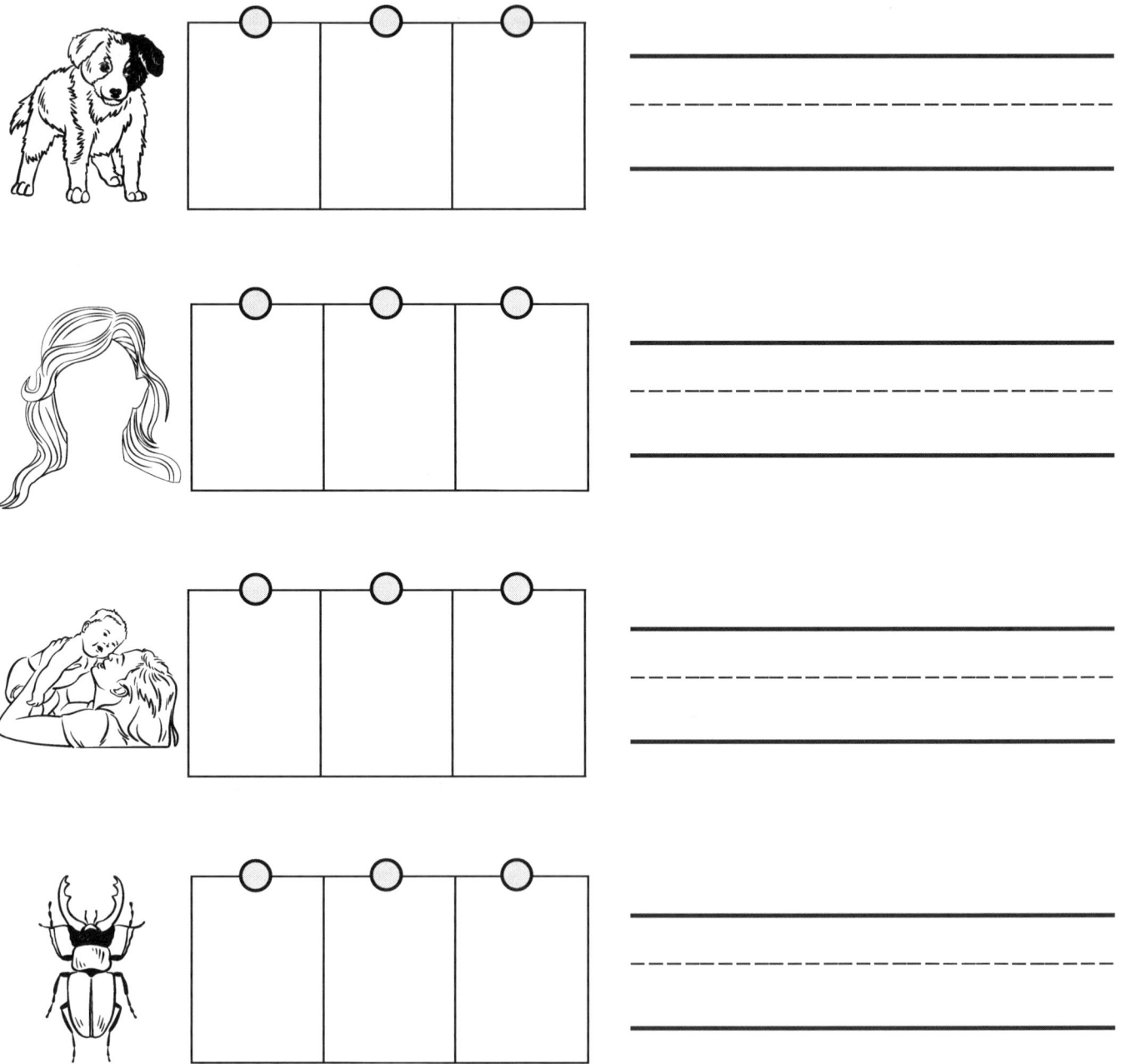

Map it, Graph it & Write it

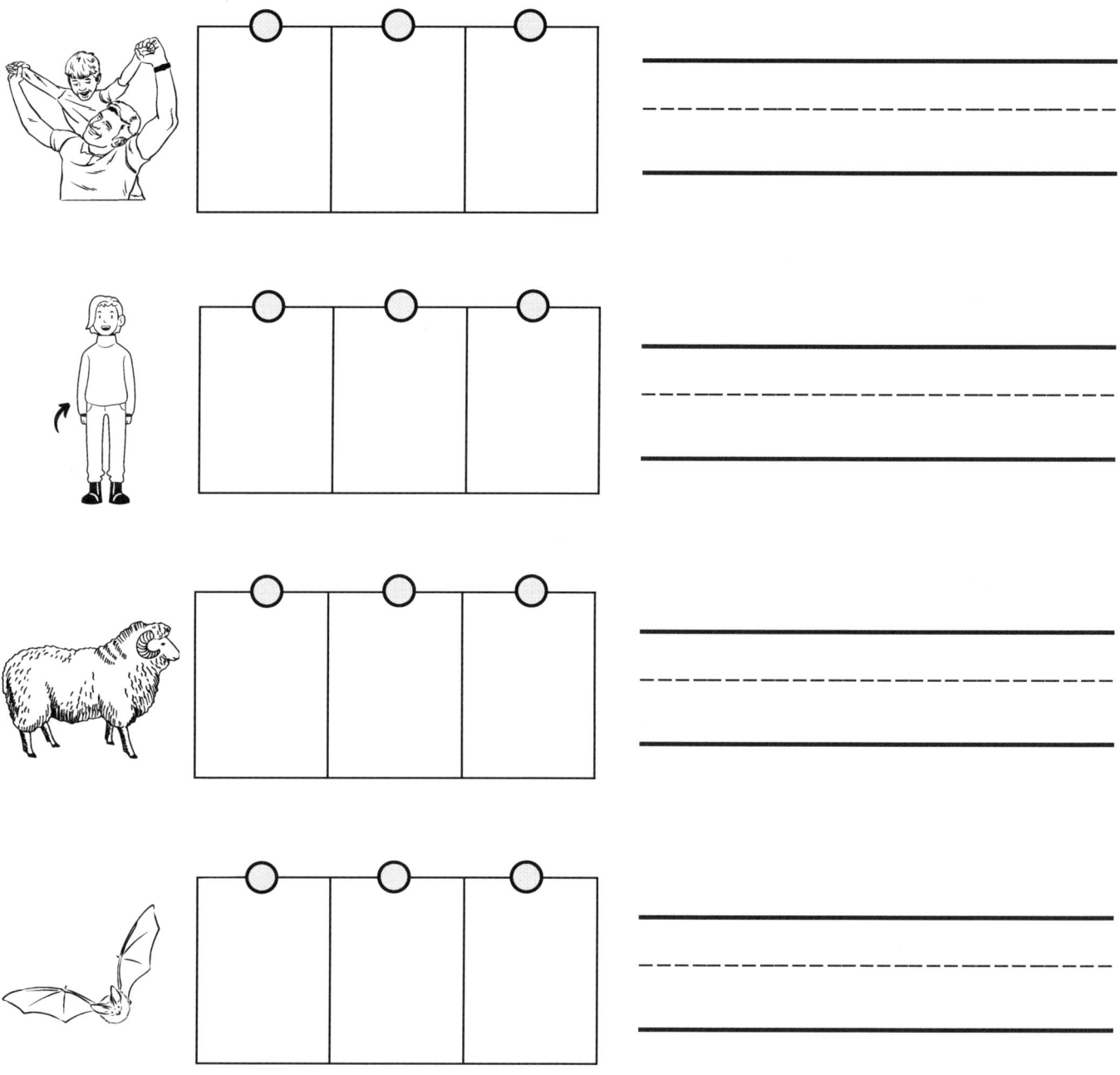

Map it, Graph it & Write it

Map it, Graph it & Write it

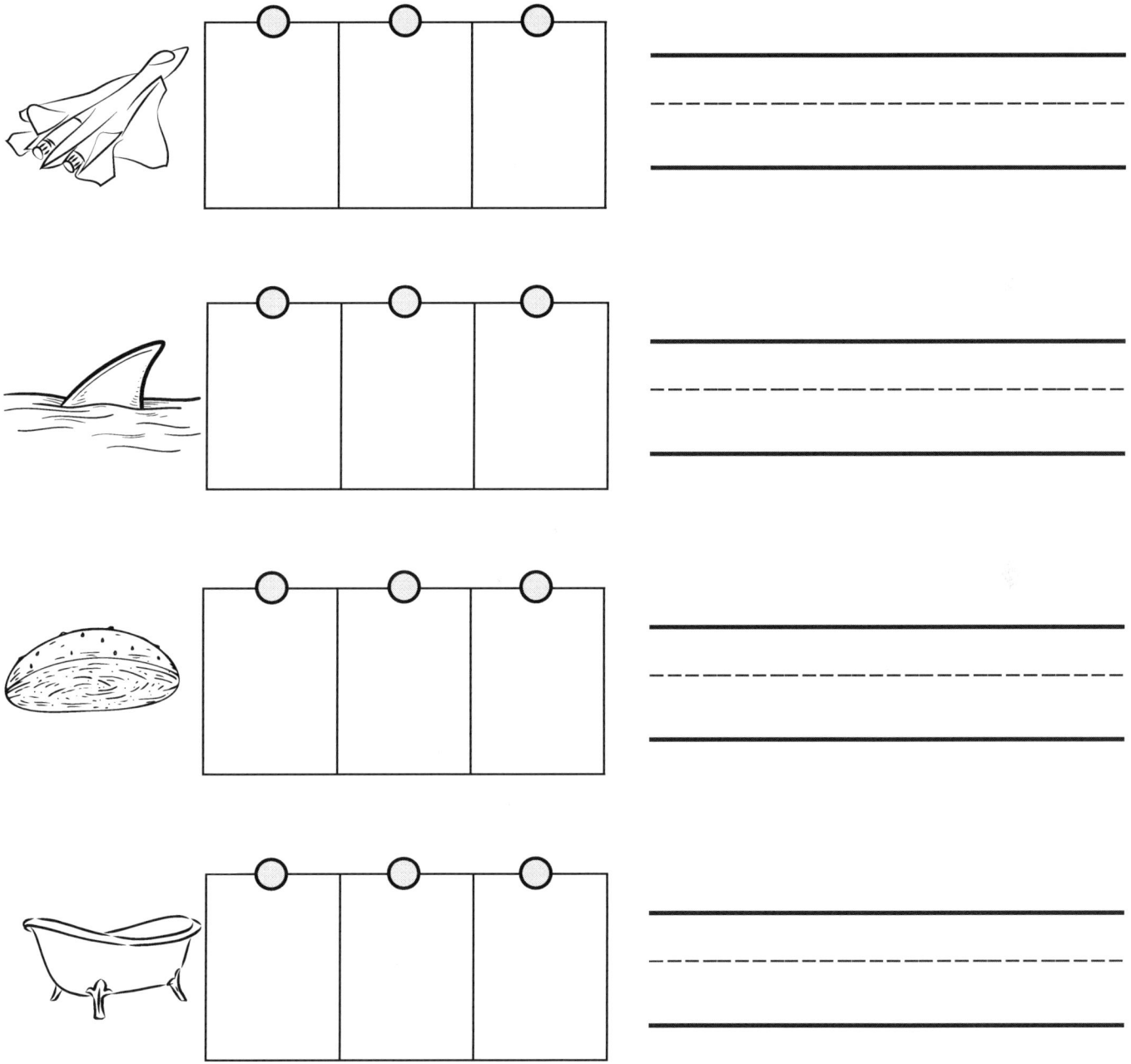

Map it, Graph it & Write it

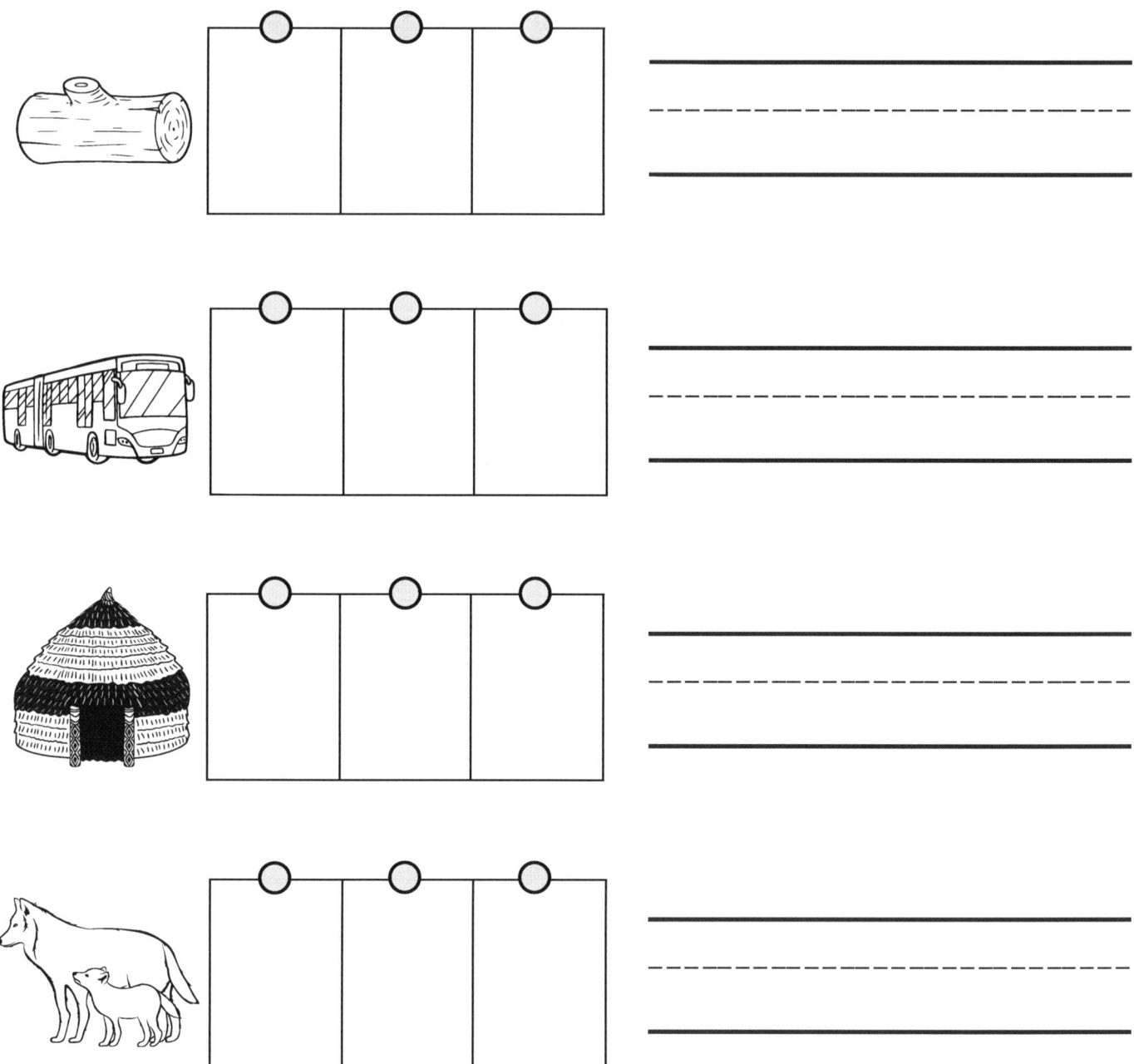

Map it, Graph it & Write it

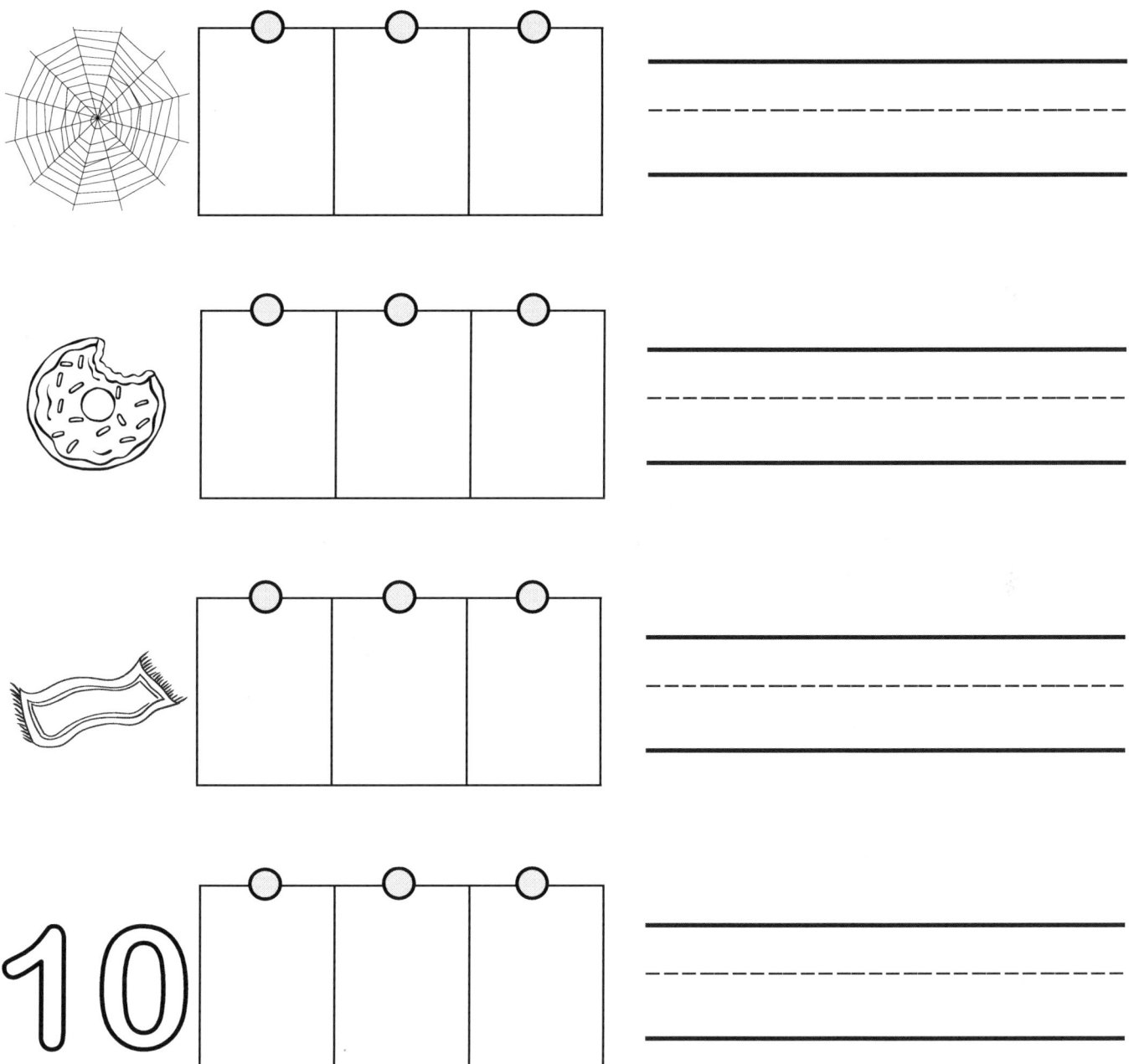

Map it, Graph it & Write it

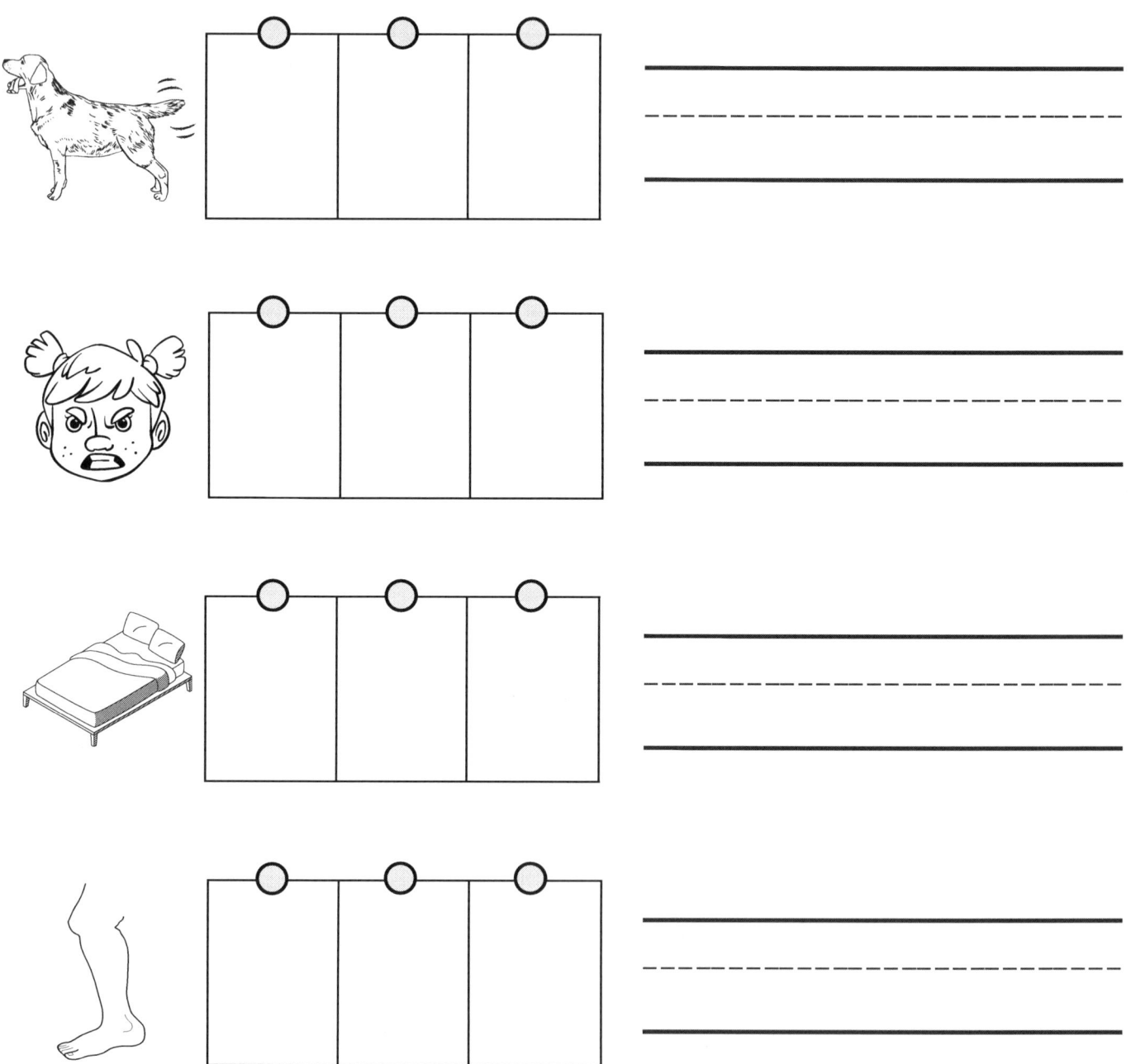

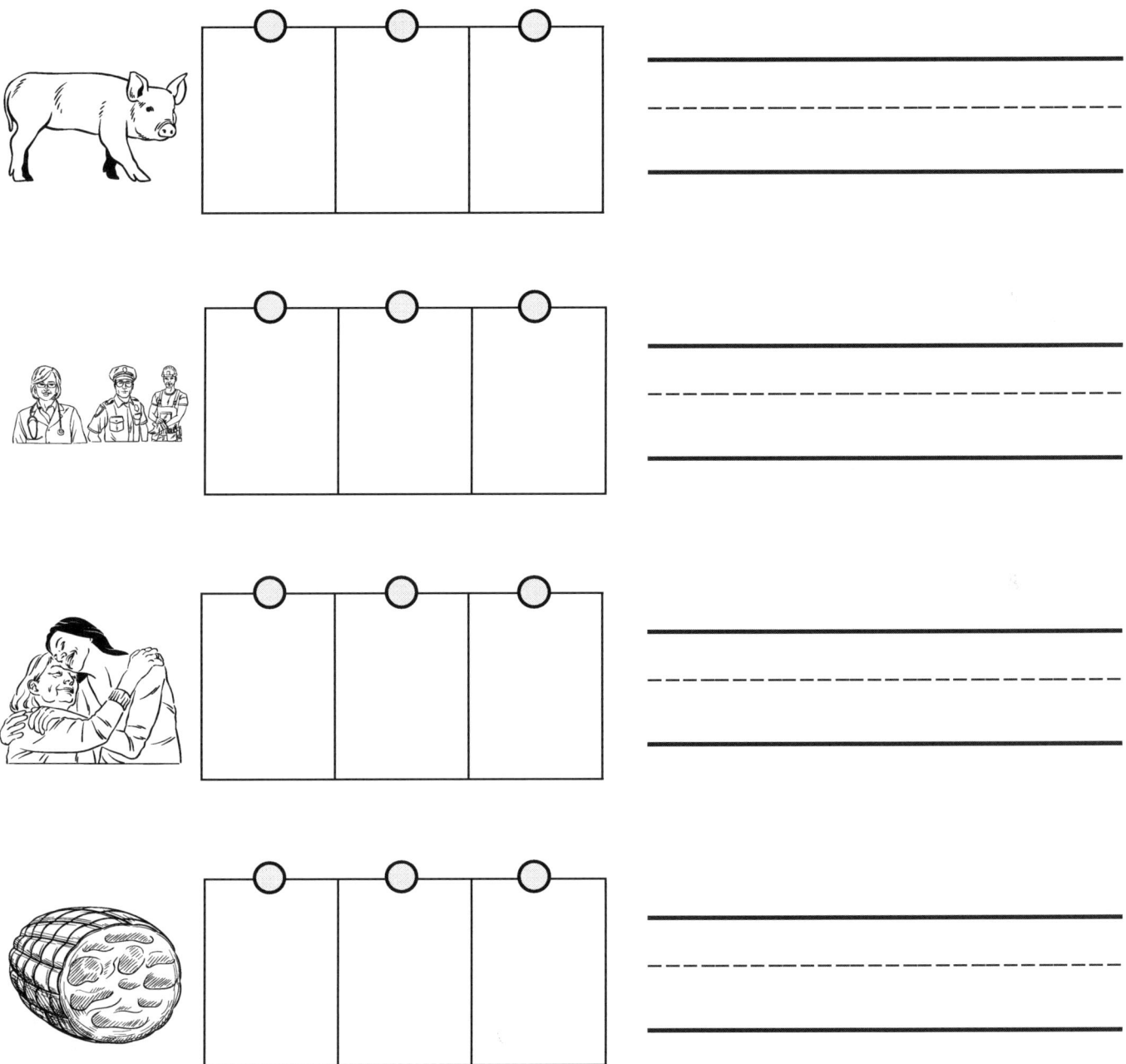

Map it, Graph it & Write it

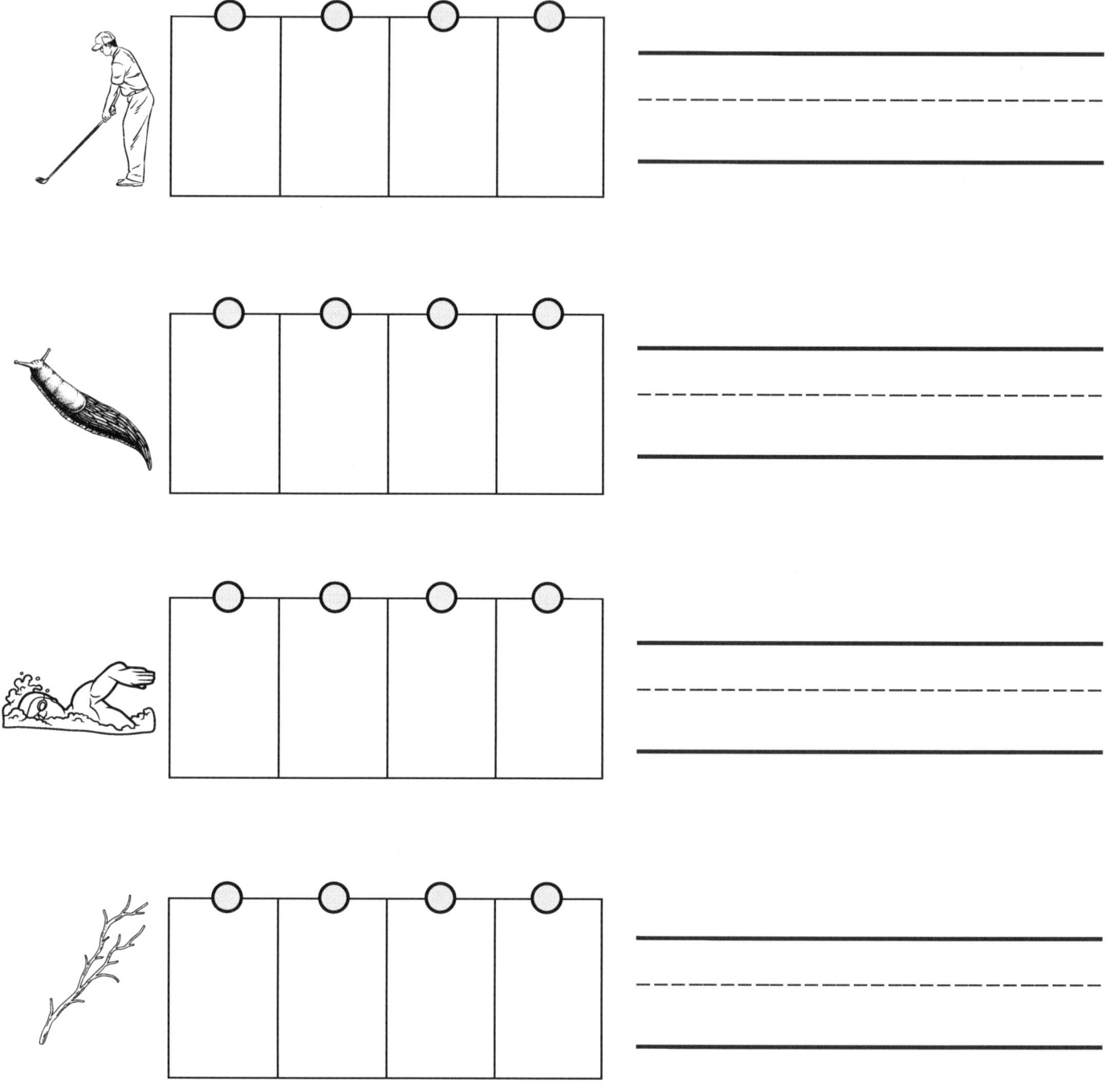

Map it, Graph it & Write it

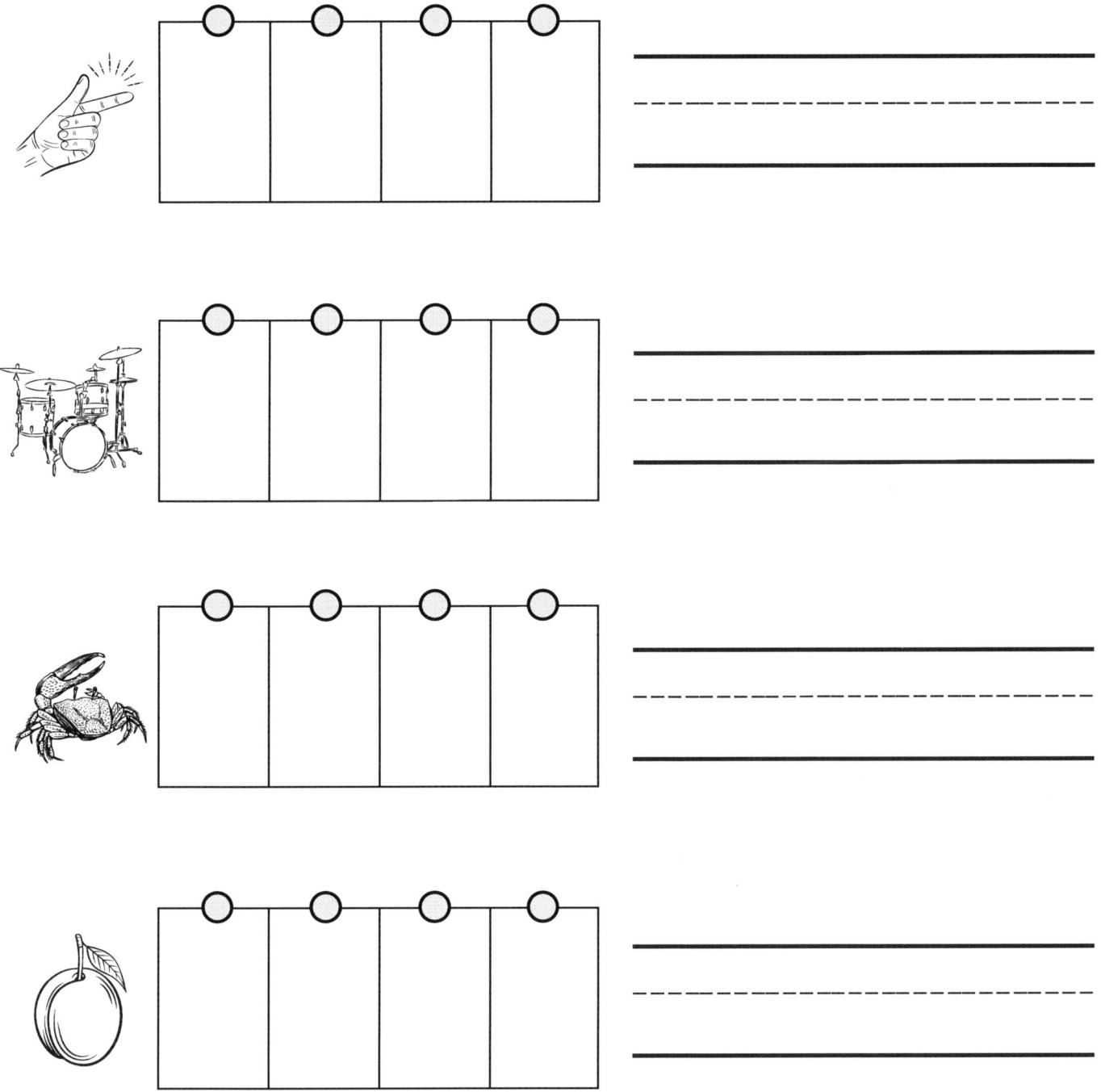

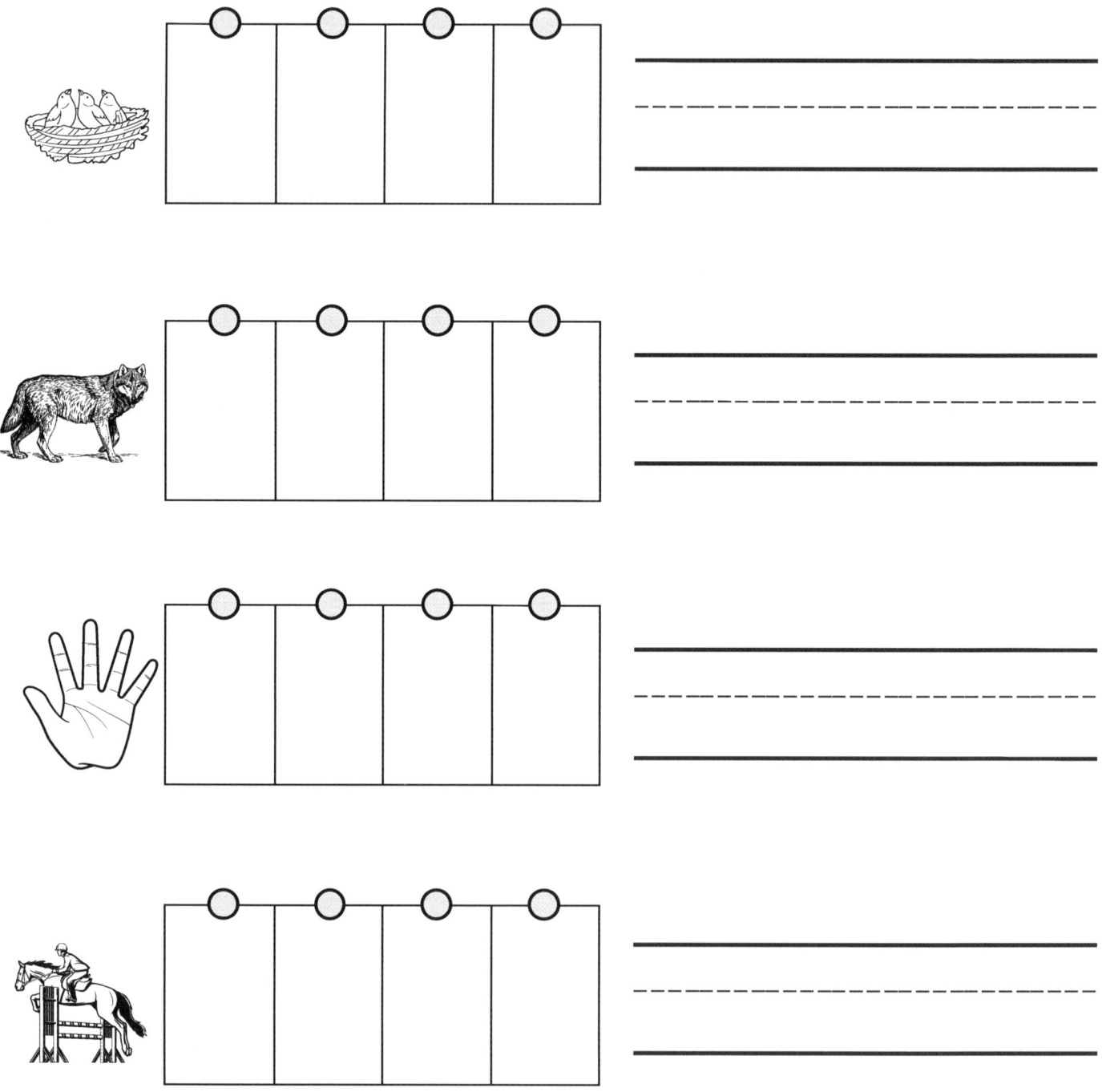

Map it, Graph it & Write it

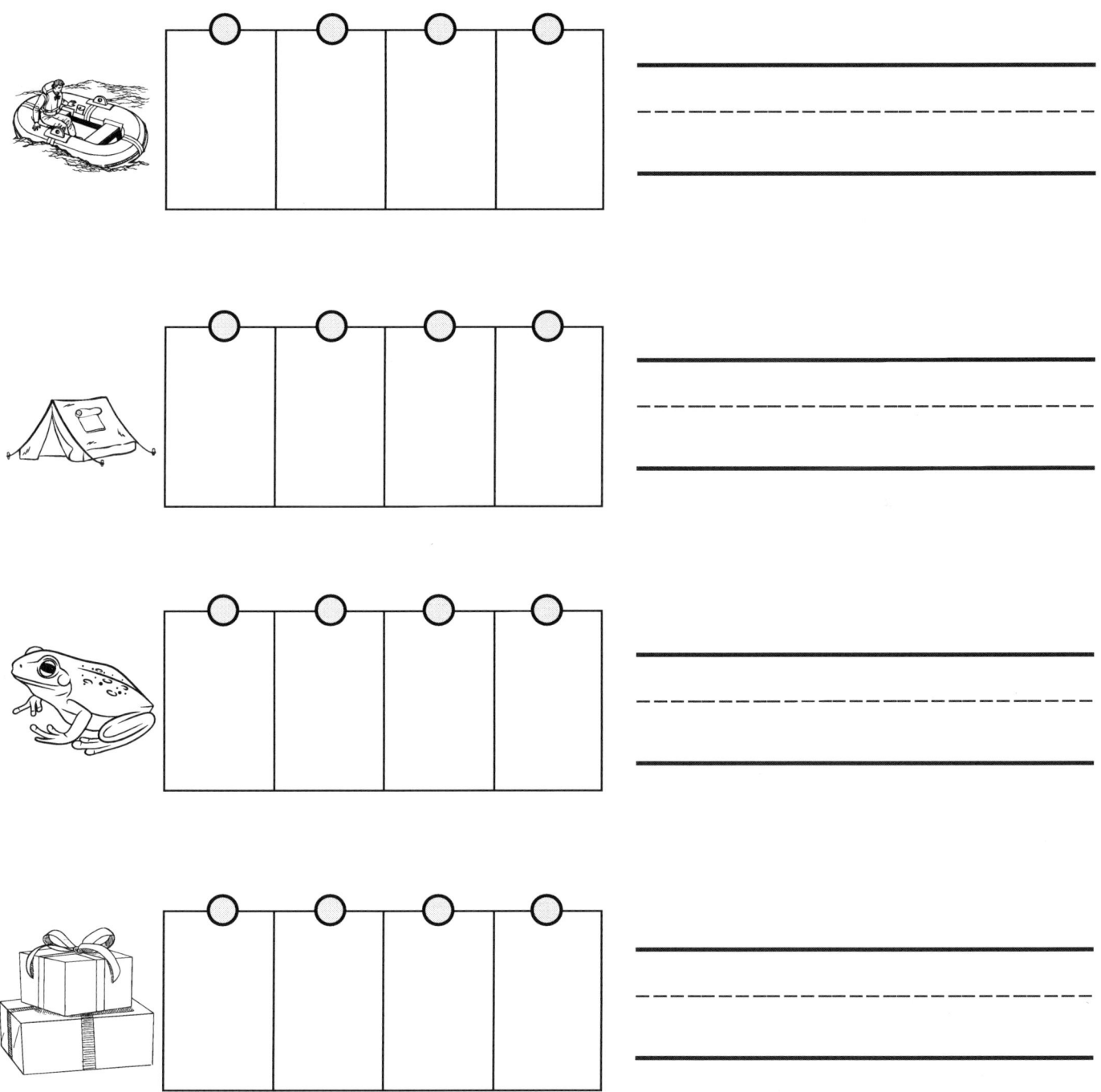

Map it, Graph it & Write it

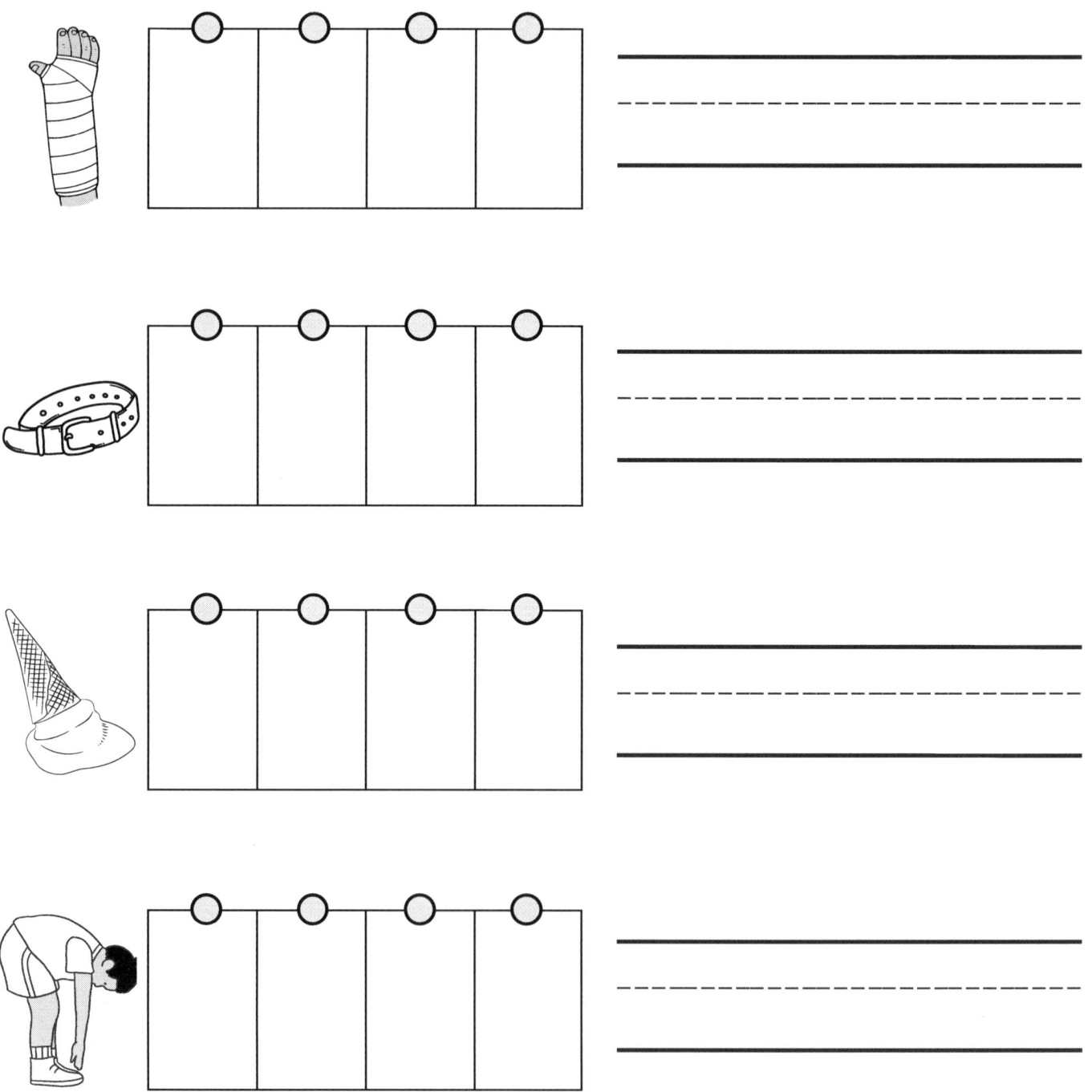

Draw a line to match the word to the image.
Match incorrect words to X.

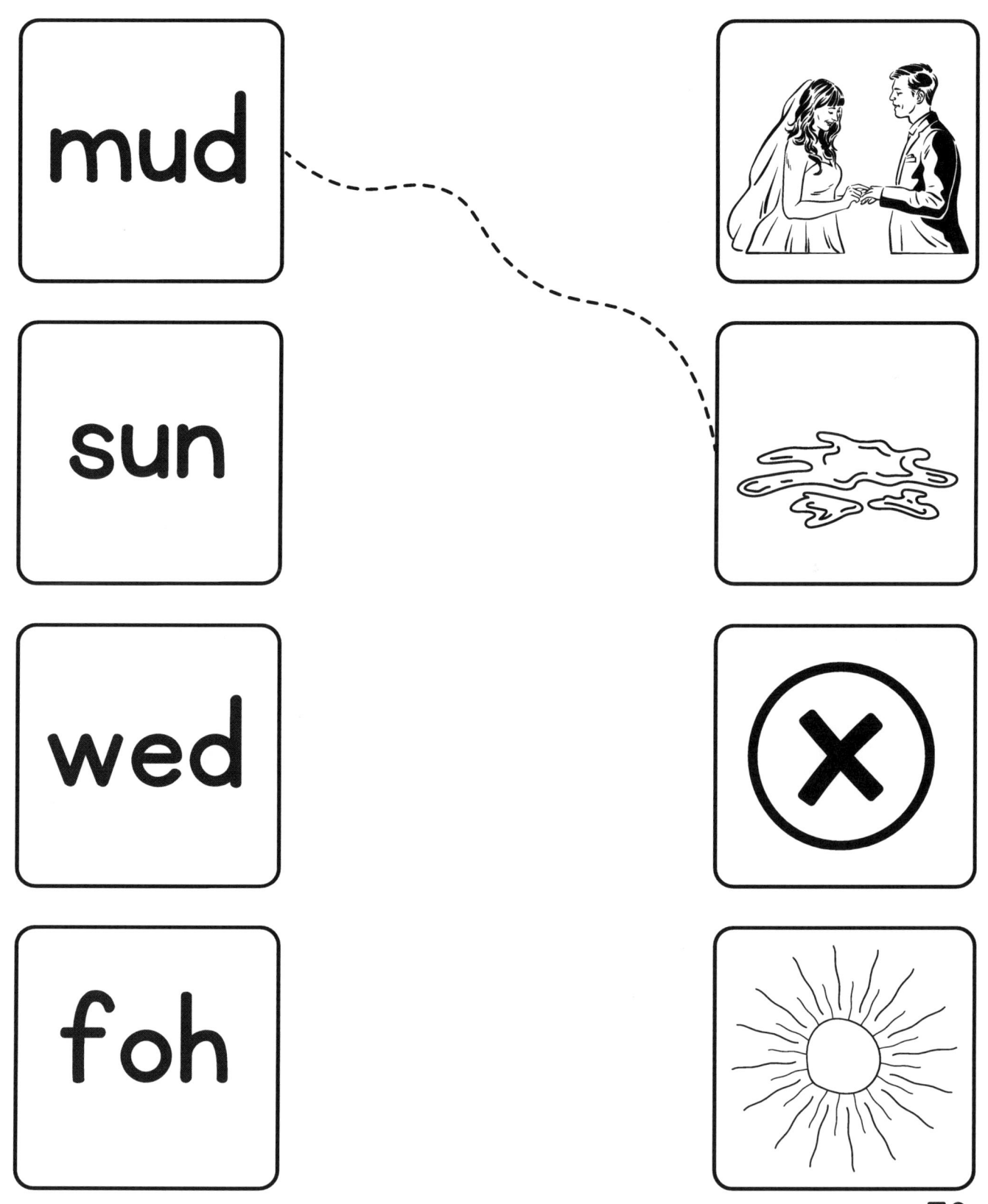

mud

sun

wed

foh

70

Draw a line to match the word to the image.

tob

ax

fun

pan

71

Draw a line to match the word to the image.

cag

bin

cat

cap

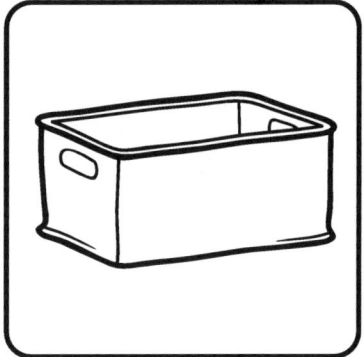

72

Draw a line to match the word to the image.

leg

box

fed

tes

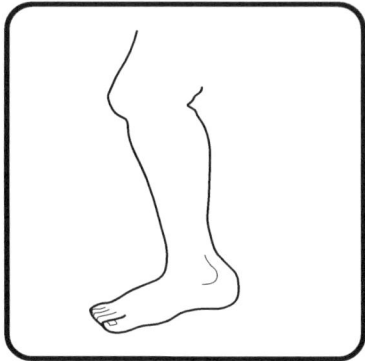

73

Draw a line to match the word to the image.

hop

hog

pit

hov

74

Draw a line to match the word to the image.

jug

pet

nel

big

Draw a line to match the word to the image.

pup

dip

vet

ral

76

Draw a line to match the word to the image.

keg

nun

lof

lab

77

Draw a line to match the word to the image.

plug

frip

slug

flag

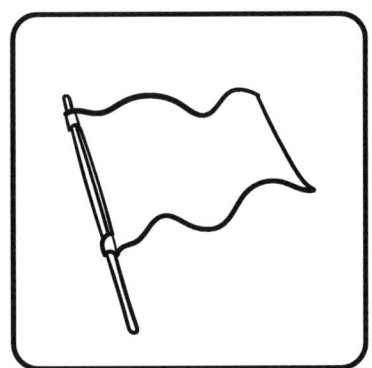

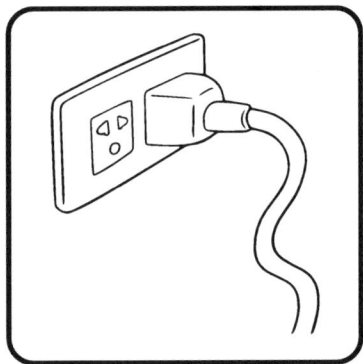

Draw a line to match the word to the image.

vest

grab

sagf

bolt

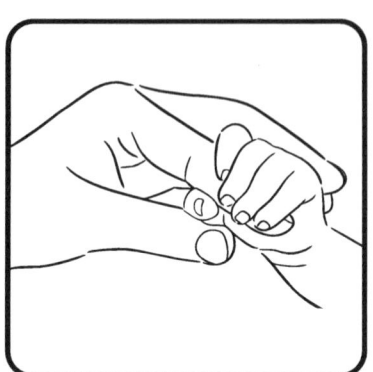

Draw a line to match the word to the image.

drift

clam

gicl

tram

80

Draw a line to match the word to the image.

jump

grin

drej

spin

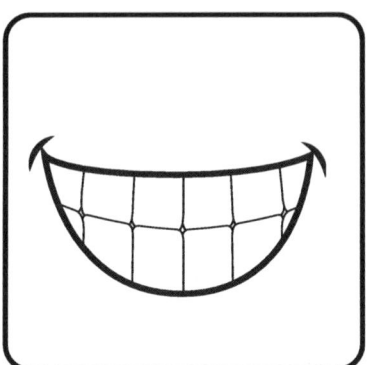

81

Draw a line to match the word to the image.

stamp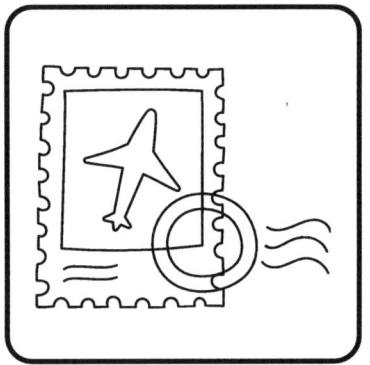

frosl

plant

crust

Draw a line to match the word to the image.

print

stump

pling

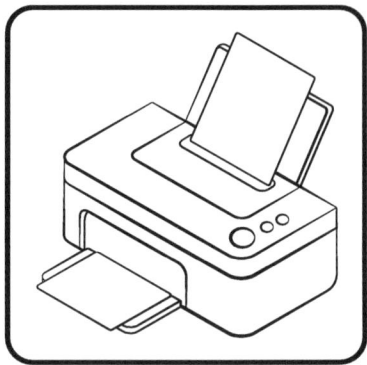

stand

83

Introduce these nine sight words to your child so that they can decode the following sentences.

the	his	has
on	is	to
he	in	a

Draw a line to match the sentence to the image.

A sad man.

A cat in a hat.

Pet a dog.

A man in a van.

The mug is hot.

Draw a line to match the sentence to the image.

Meg has dots.

A fox naps.

Bob is mad.

The cat is fat.

The pet can hop.

Draw a line to match the sentence to the image.

The frog sat on the log.

The bug is on the pot.

A tot is in the crib.

Bob wet the mop.

Sam sips on the pop.

87

Draw a line to match the sentence to the image.

The flag has a rip.

The cab has a flat.

The pig has a hat.

The drum is fun.

The cat sits on the rug.

88

Draw a line to match the sentence to the image.

The ant is on the web.

Bob will trap the rat.

The twig can snap.

The car has to stop.

Let us clap if he wins.

89

Draw a line to match the sentence to the image.

The crab can swim.

The crust is hot.

Meg put jam on the bun.

Meg will dim the lamp.

A dog jumps in the pond.

Draw a line to match the sentence to the image.

Bob cut the stump.

He has a cut on his hand.

Meg hugs her cat.

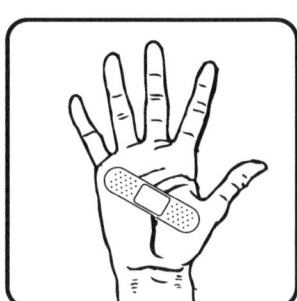

The cat hid.

The jet will land.

Draw a line to match the sentence to the image.

Pam can trim the wig.

The top can spin.

The tub is wet.

Pam is in the lab.

Dad is at his job.

Draw a line to match the sentence to the image.

The gift is in a box.

Sam has a cap.

Bob has a vest.

The fan has lots of dust.

Pam drags the sled.

Draw a line to match the sentence to the image.

The plant and the sun.

The cast can help her leg

Put the lid on the pot.

The nest has eggs.

Let's bump fists.

94

Make a check mark next to the correct sentence. Circle the
mistake in the other sentence.

	The rat is in the cap.	✓
	The rat is in the (lap).	

	The mat is on the hut.	
	The bat is on the hut.	

	The bog sat.	
	The dog sat.	

	The bug is on the stump.	
	The bug is on the bump.	

Make a check mark next to the correct sentence. Circle the
mistake in the other sentence.

	Meg san clap.	
	Meg can clap.	

	The hand has a dug.	
	The hand has a mug.	

	Pam puts on a bat.	
	Pam puts on a hat.	

	Bob can nap in a bed.	
	Bob can nap in a sled.	

Make a check mark next to the correct sentence. Circle the mistake in the other sentence.

	Drop the lip in the hand.	
	Drop the clip in the hand.	

	Tim can grab the ax.	
	Tim can crab the ax.	

	The kid is in the band.	
	The kid is in the sand.	

	Bob can camp in a tent.	
	Bob can stamp in a tent.	

Write a sentence using the words provided.

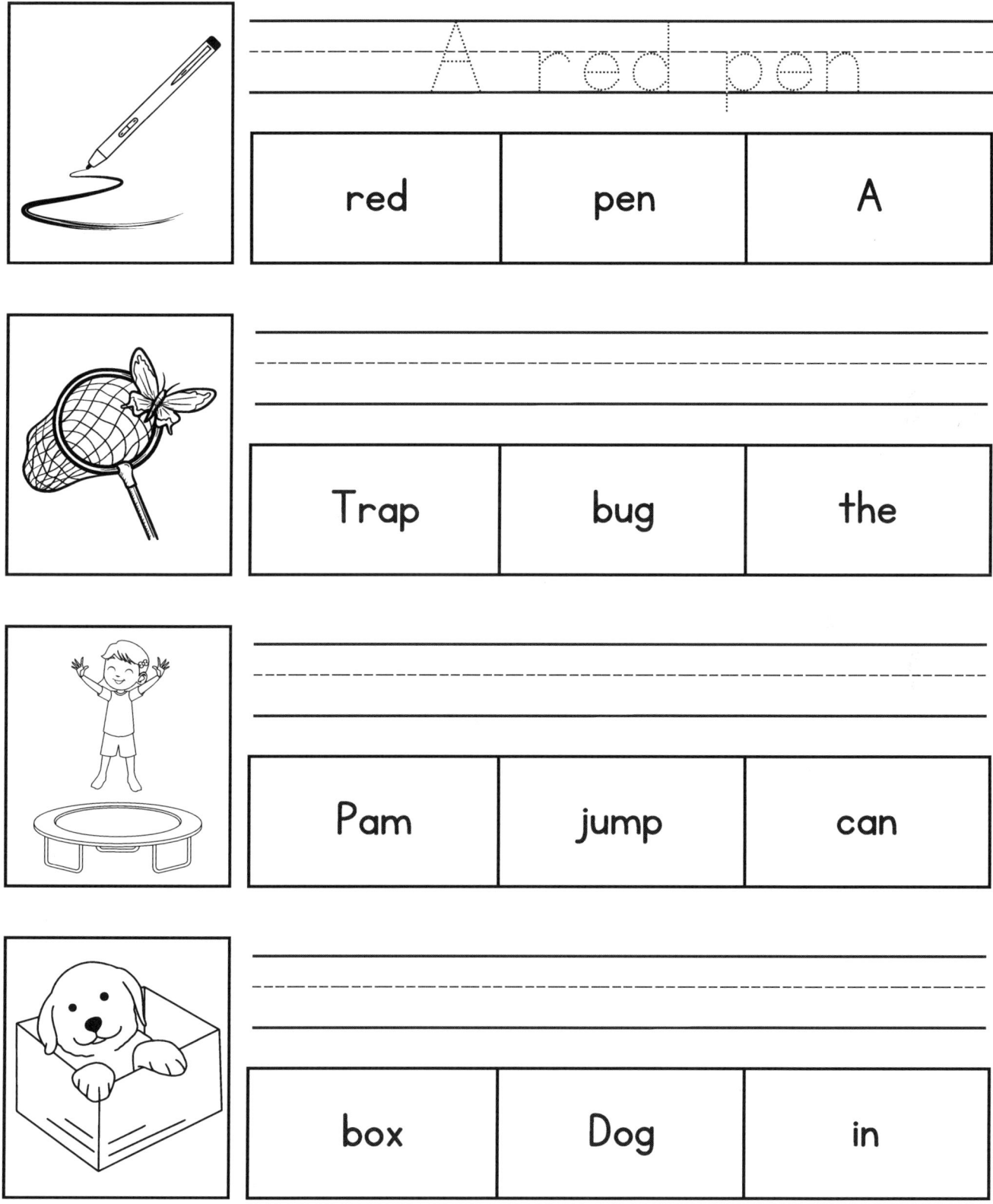

A red pen

red	pen	A

Trap	bug	the

Pam	jump	can

box	Dog	in

98

Write a sentence using the words provided.

rug	The	big	is

A	dots	pup	has

sun	is	hot	The

Tim	a	is	tot

Write a sentence using the words provided.

frog	wet	The	is

Dad	his	and	son

The	is	bus	fast

in	Eggs	the	nest

Write a sentence using the words provided.

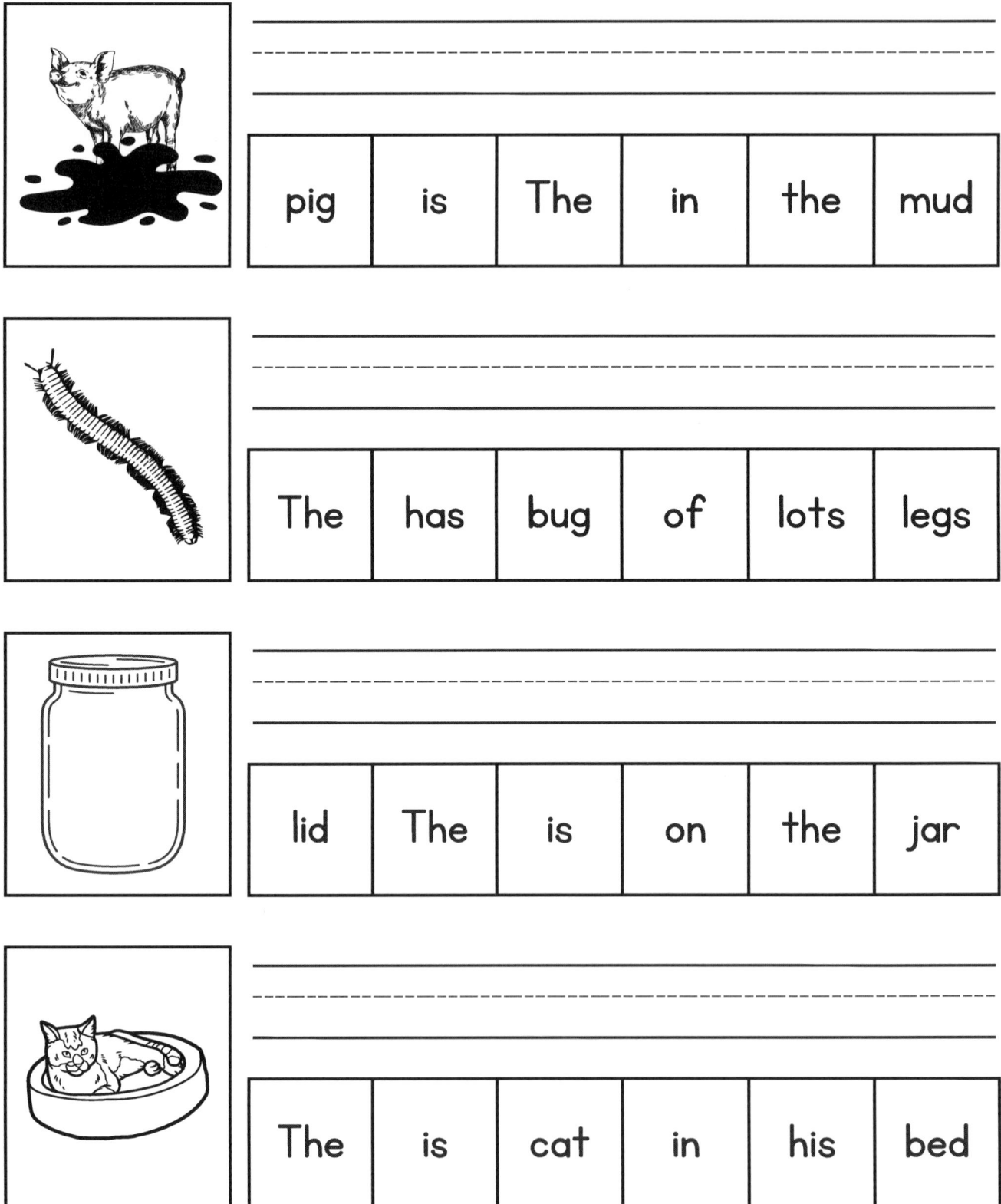

| pig | is | The | in | the | mud |

| The | has | bug | of | lots | legs |

| lid | The | is | on | the | jar |

| The | is | cat | in | his | bed |

Moveable alphabet

a	e	i	o	u
b	c	d	f	g
h	j	k	l	m
n	p	q	r	s
t	u	v	w	x
p	t	l	r	s

blank page for cut and paste

Made in United States
Orlando, FL
19 June 2025

62251556R10061